An Illustrated History of the
KENT & EAST SUSSEX
RAILWAY

An Illustrated History
of the
KENT &
EAST SUSSEX
RAILWAY

John Scott-Morgan

OPC

An imprint of
Ian Allan Publishing

First published 2007

ISBN (10) 0 86093 608 2
ISBN (13) 978 0 86093 608 4

© Ian Allan Publishing Ltd 2007

Published by Oxford Publishing Co

an imprint of Ian Allan Publishing Ltd, Hersham, Surrey, KT12 4RG
Printed in England by Ian Allan Printing Ltd, Hersham, Surrey, KT12 4RG

Code: 0702/B

Visit the Ian Allan Publishing website at www.ianallanpublishing.com

This book is dedicated to the memory of John L. Smith, who in 1967 wrote *Rails to Tenterden*, and to Charles Kentsley, Frank Davies and Sheridan R. Mazurek, three pioneers of the Kent & East Sussex Railway Association, who helped to save the line.

Front cover: On hire from the Southern Railway, ex-LBSCR Class A1X 'Terrier' 2678 emerges from Tenterden St Michael's Tunnel with a train from Headcorn Junction to Tenterden in the summer of 1947. *from a painting by Eric Bottomley*

Half-title: On hire from the Southern Railway, ex-LBSCR Class A1X 'Terrier' No 2678 stands at Headcorn Junction c1947 with a mixed train comprising an ex-LSWR Brake Composite carriage and seven cattle vans, the number of the latter suggesting that the photograph was taken during Biddenden Fair week. Note also the ex-LSWR road brake van. *Author's collection*

Title pages: Transition at Rolvenden: the first Model T Ford railbus set shortly after its arrival in 1923. The three petrol railbus sets delivered to the Kent & East Sussex Railway — two Fords and one Shefflex — represented an attempt to cut running costs, necessitated by a drop in receipts after World War 1. *Lens of Sutton collection*

Left: Ex-LSWR saddle tank E0334 (KESR No 4) at Robertsbridge Junction c1936, showing a good view from the smokebox end. No 4 was later re-boilered using a Drummond boiler. Note the stone-crushing plant in the background. *C. Hamilton Ellis*

Right: Cast-iron KESR plate on 'Terrier' No 3, photographed in July 1939. *R. F. Roberts*

Contents

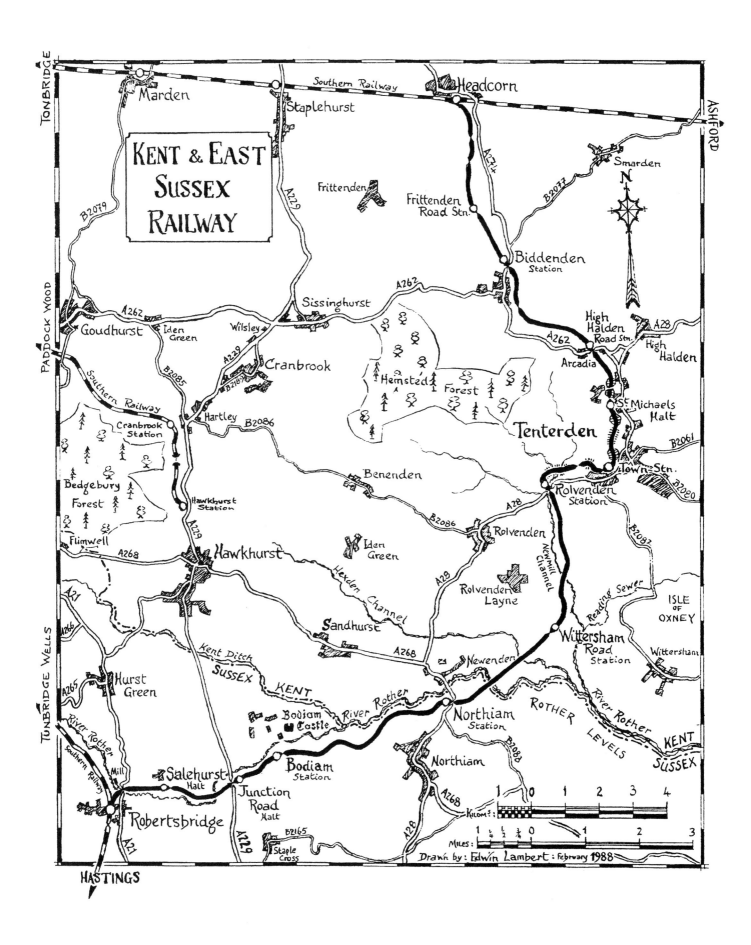

KENT & EAST
SUSSEX
RAILWAY

Drawn by: Edwin Lambert: February 1988

Introduction

The Kent & East Sussex Railway was one of Britain's most famous light railways. Part of Colonel Stephens' empire of minor railways, it was reputedly his favourite, and this is substantiated by the time and money he spent on it, at least in the early years.

The history of the line is long and complicated, for the concept of building a railway to Tenterden originated in the 1850s with the South Eastern Railway projecting a series of branch lines from the London–Dover main line to Tenterden, then an important market town. The first of two principal SER projects involved a branch from Headcorn to Tenterden via Biddenden, with an option to continue to Appledore, which would have provided a link with a proposed new port at Dungeness. The second, less ambitious project was to construct a line from Cranbrook, on the Paddock Wood and Hawkhurst line, using the alignment proposed subsequently by the Kent & East Sussex Railway for its Cranbrook extension to reach a point close to the site of Rolvenden station (the original Tenterden station); this would also have allowed the possibility of continuing to Appledore and the South Kent coast.

The SER and its Chairman, Sir Edward Watkins, played a long-running game with the people of Tenterden, for despite having Parliamentary approval to construct both lines they had no intention of doing so. Sir Edward and the SER Board were too involved in the project to build the Channel Tunnel and in long-term plans to link a number of northern railways with London (via the Metropolitan Railway) and Paris (via the SER and the proposed tunnel). This situation continued until the late 1890s, by which time the people of Tenterden were becoming exasperated by the lack of activity and by the lapse of a number of Acts permitting the construction of a branch to the town.

The construction by the SER of the branch from Paddock Wood to Cranbrook and Hawkhurst was, for some local worthies, the last straw, the branch serving a number of villages of lesser importance than Tenterden. What they did not know was that the SER also had plans for a line from Hawkhurst to Appledore or Rye, which it felt would be financially more viable than a line through Tenterden. The people of Tenterden would finally get their railway, but not quite in the form — or from the direction — they had always envisaged throughout the long years of deliberating over the project.

One of the young engineers involved in the Paddock Wood–Hawkhurst project was one Holman Fred Stephens, who had worked closely with Consulting Engineer Edward Seaton and could see the need for improved transport in the Weald of Kent. Born in Hammersmith, London, in 1868, Stephens was educated in England and Germany before embarking, in 1895, on an engineering career during the final period of British railway development. During the course of his training he worked on the Metropolitan Railway at Neasden, under the direction of J. J. Hanbury, and would very likely have visited the Brill Tramway in Buckinghamshire, which line was operated for its owner, the Duke of Buckingham, under a lease agreement.

Stephens was a great promoter of the Light Railway Bill, enacted 1896, which encouraged the construction of lightly constructed lines to serve areas not covered by the existing network. In particular, he and his backers promoted a line, to be known as the Rother Valley Railway, to link Robertsbridge and Tenterden via Bodiam and Northiam — a distance of 12 miles. The enabling Act was also passed in 1896, and the line was constructed between 1898 and 1900.

Right:
Lt Col Holman Fred Stephens, 1868-1931. Engineer and Manager of the line from its construction until his death in October 1931, he is pictured in full military uniform c1914. *Col Stephens Museum*

the first public train ran up the 1-in-50 incline to Tenterden Town station. At the same time it was announced that the company had negotiated an agreement with the South Eastern & Chatham Railway to build a line from Headcorn to Tenterden, the SECR guaranteeing to make good any losses incurred by the RVR in its operation.

More substantially built than the original Rother Valley section, the Headcorn extension was opened to the public on 15 May 1905. By this time, however, the Rother Valley Railway as a legal entity had ceased to exist, having been renamed with effect from 1 June 1904 as the Kent & East Sussex Railway.

In 1906 a Light Railway Order was obtained for the construction of a line to link Headcorn with Maidstone, as the Headcorn & Maidstone Junction Light Railway, running via Sutton Valence and Tovil and with running rights into Maidstone West station. However, although some land was purchased, no actual work commenced on what would undoubtedly have been a difficult project.

We begin our journey along the line at Robertsbridge, where the company had its own bay platform; the goods yard was shared with the Southern Railway, which owned the goods shed. The joint goods yard radiated out on the eastern side of the station. The Kent & East Sussex Railway, however, had no run-round facilities at Robertsbridge station, having to back trains out into the reception yard to run round.

Above:
The opening timetable for the Rother Valley section from Robertsbridge Junction to the first Tenterden station, which would be renamed Rolvenden after the line opened to Tenterden Town.
P. A. Harding collection

Below:
The cover of the 1902 winter timetable book, announcing the imminent opening of the line to Tenterden Town station.
Author's collection

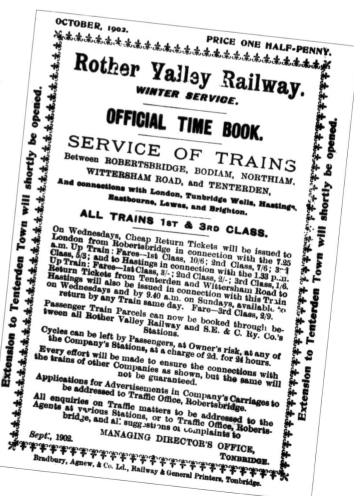

Despite the clamour locally for a railway serving an area ignored by the SER for more than 50 years the burghers of Tenterden were still hoping for a line from the Headcorn direction, many of them caring little for a long branch from Robertsbridge that terminated a mile and a half south of their town, at the foot of a steep hill. Thus the RVR Board lacked ready funds, which situation frequently led to fraught negotiations with the contractors, and the line was ultimately completed by the company itself. The railway from Robertsbridge to that first station at Tenterden finally opened for goods traffic on 26 March 1900 and to passengers a week later, on 2 April.

At every stage the RVR was short of finance, and this resulted not only in the protracted construction period but also in the need to hire its first locomotives (a pair of 2-4-0 tank engines built 1899 by Hawthorn Leslie) and rolling stock. A year after opening it took delivery of a third locomotive (a 'Terrier' 0-6-0T built by the London, Brighton & South Coast Railway in 1872), purchased with the aid of a loan from Barclay's Bank and carrying plates to that effect.

Stephens and the Board had plans to expand the RVR in new directions, the main thrust being projected lines from Robertsbridge to Pevensey (16 miles), from Northiam to Rye (9 miles) and from Rolvenden to Cranbrook (10 miles), but the lack of capital meant that these never came to fruition. However, the plan to extend the existing line by 1½ miles from its original terminus south of the town into Tenterden proper was realised on 16 March 1903, when

After leaving Robertsbridge the line turned sharply to the east, on a steep incline that descended to a level crossing at Hudson's Mill. Here the Kent & East Sussex Railway had sidings that ran into the mill for the flour traffic. From here the line ran level for 10 miles or so, passing Salehurst Halt, Junction Road Halt and Bodiam and Northiam stations. The halt at Salehurst consisted

of only a sleeper-built platform, while that at Junction Road had a concrete platform that had replaced an earlier timber structure; neither had any buildings. At Bodiam was built a typical Colonel Stephens station, with a corrugated-iron building with wooden awning supported by three wooden pillars with struts at the top. All the stations on the line had men's lavatories only. Both Bodiam and Junction Road served the local hop farms.

Three and a half miles on from Bodiam was Northiam, outwardly similar but with a run-round loop and originally a second platform, which was later removed. From here the line crossed the River Rother via a 66ft-span bridge that took it from East Sussex into Kent and Wittersham Road. This station had its buildings at a right-angle to the platform and lacked an awning. Across Potmans Heath and due north was Rolvenden, the original Tenterden station. Here the company had its workshops and locomotive shed. From here the line ascended a 1-in-50 incline to Tenterden Town station, located on the west of the town, 14 miles from Robertsbridge. Quite unlike the other stations on the line, Tenterden Town was a brick building with two platforms. It was also the line's halfway point, at which trains from both Robertsbridge and Headcorn terminated; the railway from Tenterden Town to Headcorn was regarded as a completely separate extension line.

The Headcorn extension, opened to traffic in 1905, had features quite different from those on the Rother Valley section, the stations being built of timber rather than corrugated iron or brick. However, all the platforms were constructed of brick or timber.

The section from Tenterden Town to Tenterden St Michael's Halt ran through the back of the town. At St Michael's there was a timber-and-brick platform with a small building. Also at this point the line ran through a short tunnel. North of here the railway ran through stations at High Halden Road, Biddenden, where there was a loop and a second platform, and Frittenden Road before arriving at Headcorn Junction, where the platform was on a curve. The railway's mileage to this point was 21½ miles. The northern part of the line served the hop fields and farming communities of southern Kent.

Station Road, Bodiam.

(1) KENT & EAST SUSSEX RAILWAY TRAIN.

A series of postcards produced by the KESR in 1905 depicting attractions to be found along the line.

(2) BODIAM CASTLE AND MOAT (BODIAM STATION).

(3) BRICKWALL HOUSE (NORTHIAM STATION).

(4) ROLVENDEN HIGH STREET (ROLVENDEN STATION).

(5) TENTERDEN, OLD HOUSES IN HIGH STREET (TENTERDEN TOWN STATION).

(6) CLOTHWORKERS' HALL (BIDDENDEN STATION).

11

Signalling on the line consisted of a mixture of wooden-posted lower-quadrant types and some rail-built upper-quadrant signals at Robertsbridge and Headcorn Junction. There were, however, some odds and ends. At Tenterden Town station was a unique three-arm signal on a lattice post, while at High Halden Road and Wittersham Road were equally odd slotted signals, each with a double arm; a similar type with two arms on different parts of the post was to be found at Frittenden Road. At Rolvenden there were small shunt signals on short posts located near the large water tower. Most of the stations had home starter signals at each end of the approach lines from Robertsbridge and Headcorn. At Biddenden there was a ground-level shunt signal, used to control access to the goods yard.

The permanent way used on both the Rother Valley section and the line through to Headcorn Junction varied between the original flat-bottom rail, dog-spiked to wooden sleepers, to ex-SER double-headed bullhead rail. However, by the mid-1940s the entire railway had been re-laid with 90lb bullhead rail, to enable the line to be used as an alternative route in case of emergencies; some of the bullhead rail came from the closed Elham Valley branch in Kent.

Right:
A young William Henry Austen, Manager of the KESR from 1931 until nationalisation in 1948. He had worked with the Colonel from their first meeting during construction of the Hawkhurst line in the 1890s. Austen died in 1956. *Col Stephens Museum*

Below:
The hub of the Colonel's empire: 23 Salford Terrace, Tonbridge, Kent. Situated near Tonbridge railway station, this was the general office that administered all the Colonel's light railways, including the KESR. This photograph, taken on 21 September 1936, shows the front entrance, with signboard listing all the lines managed within. *J. H. L. Adams*

Along the line there were wind pumps to raise water for the water towers, examples of which existed at Robertsbridge, Headcorn, Tenterden and Rolvenden; in later years the company used the Southern water tower at Robertsbridge. Also at Robertsbridge was a water crane, again an SR facility, being an ex-SER double type, with two hoses. At Rolvenden the company had a rather makeshift-looking example, which survived until very recently. At Tenterden there was a small water tank next to the three-arm signal. The facility provided at Headcorn was located about half a mile south of the station and consisted of a collection of water tanks and a wind pump, which was still in use in British Railways days. At one time a similar facility had existed at Robertsbridge.

Over the years the company owned an incredible collection of locomotives and rolling stock. The former included second-hand Brighton 'Terriers', a collection of second-hand saddle tanks and some new equipment built when the line was opened. The rolling stock consisted of four-wheel and bogie carriages. In addition the railway ran a fleet of petrol railbuses in the 1920s and 1930s. The line also had a fleet of new and second-hand goods wagons.

The company did moderately well in its early years, returning modest profits prior to the outbreak of World War 1. Thereafter it went into a decline that would see it pass into receivership in 1932. By this time control had passed to W. H. Austen, Col Stephens having died in October 1931. Austen had been the Colonel's loyal assistant from the early days, having worked in the Tonbridge office that ran his empire of light railways, and, although he lacked the Colonel's high-flying connections, he undoubtedly had an ability to manage them in a more practical way.

Where the KESR was concerned Austen came to arrangement with Southern Railway General Manager Sir Herbert Walker whereby the SR would defray some of the cost of disposing of redundant rolling-stock and would supply serviceable replacements. Thus time-expired KESR four- and six-wheel carriages were replaced in the late 1930s by recently withdrawn ex-LSWR non-corridor bogie stock as replacements, while the early 1940s saw the arrival of two ex-LSWR corridor brakes that would serve the KESR until the early 1950s. The line also benefitted from the hire of small tanks (normally from Classes A1X and P) and tender locomotives (Class O1 and 0395); this permitted the KESR's worn-out locomotives — of which there were many rotting in the sidings at Rolvenden — to be cut for scrap, and following the outbreak in 1939 of World War 2 the remainder of the line's derelict locomotives and rolling-stock was disposed of as part of the wartime scrap drive.

During the early part of the war the KESR found itself in the front line and was protected by an Army unit with a rail-mounted gun based at Rolvenden. The unit used ex-GWR 'Dean Goods' locomotives owned by the War Department and was manned by the Royal Engineers and the Royal Artillery, although it was unable to prevent St Michael's Tunnel at Tenterden from being strafed by an enemy raider, which inflicted significant damage on one of the portals. In the build-up to D-Day sections of pipe for PLUTO (Pipe Line Under The Ocean — to supply the Allies with fuel following the landings) passed beneath the line at various locations, while goods trains would frequently run day and night to relieve other lines in the area. It must have come as a sight for sore eyes when, on 8 May 1945 (VE Day), rebuilt 'Terrier' No 3 emerged in fully lined apple green, decked with bunting and Union flags.

The continuing austerity of the immediate postwar era led to the nationalisation of the railways, which took effect on 1 January 1948. On the KESR improvements were made to the track and stations, but, absorbed into the vast organisation that

Above:
An early enamel 'Trespass' notice c1935. *Lens of Sutton collection*

was British Railways, the line somehow lost much of its vibrance and vitality. As early as 1948 there were moves afoot to rid BR of this Edwardian relic, which was something of an enigma to the officials at Waterloo. In the event the KESR lasted six years into nationalisation as a passenger line, closing to passenger traffic on 2 January 1954, after which the section between Headcorn Junction and Tenterden Town station was lifted; the rest of the line continued as a freight-only operation until 12 June 1961, when it too closed. Today the section between Tenterden Town and Bodiam, taken over in 1962 by the Kent & East Sussex Railway Preservation Society, has been restored as a tourist line, the first section to be reopened, from Tenterden Town to Rolvenden, returning to life in 1974. Additionally there are plans in hand to reopen the line between Bodiam and Robertsbridge Junction, which if successful will see the original Rother Valley line, plus its extension to the second station at Tenterden, completely restored.

Below:
A postwar Austen cast 'Trespass' notice at Rolvenden yard c1956. *David Lawrence*

ACKNOWLEDGEMENTS

Thanks are due to the following for the photographs used in this book:
J. Adams, J. N. Aston, R. Barnard, Roger Carpenter, S. Cartwright, H. C. Casserley, R. K. Cope, T. J. Edgington, C. Hamilton Ellis, Peter Harding, G. A. Hookham, W. M. J. Jackson, David Knapman, N. R. Knight, D. Lawrence, Nick Lera, The Rev A. W. Mace, Tom Middlemass, R. F. Roberts, Philip Shaw, N. Simmons, J. L. Smith, Adrian Vaughan, the Col Stephens Museum, the Historical Model Railway Society (HMRS) collection, LCGB / Ken Nunn collection, Lens of Sutton collection, Pamlin Prints and Photos from the Fifties. Station drawings and track diagrams by kind permission of BRB (Residuary) Ltd. Special thanks go also to Claire Turnbull and Chris Martin, for typing the original manuscript.

John Scott-Morgan
Woking
January 2007

Note:
In a number of cases it has proved impossible to ascertain the photographer's identity, and such photographs are credited to the Author's collection. Anyone wishing to claim copyright for a particular photograph is invited to contact the publisher.

Above:
First steps towards preservation. Before the line formally reopened, the Kent & East Sussex Railway Association was allowed to run the occasional train for its members only. Preserved 'Terrier' No 3 is seen on arrival at Tenterden Town station on Easter Monday (11 April) 1966. *Stanley Creer*

Right:
Poem that appeared in *Punch* magazine in 1948, with illustrations by renowned cartoonist Rowland Emitt.

BIBLIOGRAPHY

Kent & East Sussex Railway by M. Lawson Finch (published privately in 1948)

The Kent & East Sussex Railway by D. Cole (Union Publications, 1962)

The Kent & East Sussex Railway by S. R. Garratt (Oakwood Press, 1972, 1987, 1999)

Rails to Tenterden by J. L. Smith (published privately in 1967)

Tenterden Terrier, journal of the Kent & East Sussex Railway
The Colonel, journal of the Colonel Stephens Society
Original documents in the National Archives at Kew

FARMERS' TRAIN

The Kent and East Sussex Line

Ever seen a railway train
wheel deep in the wheat?
Poppies on the boiler dome:
wreaths of meadow-sweet
twined about the driving wheel—
burnished brass and polished steel:
puffs of steam like woolly lambs,
on the line to Bodiam?

His chimney's tall and thin and crowned
with a bell-mouthed top,
brassbound
all round.
He's painted green like new spring grass
and he's always pausing
at the level crossing
to let the farm carts pass.

He sees real trains at Headcorn Halt,
where he's rather shy
as they thunder by
from lordly London to the Coast.
For they're very long
and he's very short,
and he wonders if they give him a thought:
but at Methersham you ll hear him boast
that his very best mate's
the eleven-eight—
the Dover Express that's never late.

But—
as soon as he gets out of sight
of the Main Line with its metals bright
then once again
he becomes THE TRAIN
and there's pride and swank
in every puff, as he goes chuff, chuff,
with a piercing whistle now and then
(Get out of the way, you silly hen)
on his lordly way
to Newenden.

He puffs past farms,
he steams past barns,
to the Biddenden maids he tells tall yarns.
He's a snorting giant
at Freezing Hill,
he whistles the miller
at Northiam Mill,
he puffs the day's news
at the crossing gate
and says what a shame he's
five minutes late!
and snorts of course
it's the Main Line's fault!

He carries grain and he carries hops.
Wherever you hail him, there he Stops!
in fact he's a friendly sort of train.
He takes out shopping farmers' wives:
he carries a load of bees in hives:
and he carries pigs,
and oats
and goats
and several boxes of lollipops
for the village kids
at the village shops.

He knows the Marsh and he knows the Weald,
he knows each wood and he knows each field:
with his bright green paint
and his glistening brass:
the rabbits stop
to see him pass.
And Arcadia's just another station
on his twice-a-daily
pere-
grination!

A trip along the line

Robertsbridge Junction

Left:
A sleepy afternoon at Robertsbridge Junction, Saturday 8 July 1939. Taken (from the footbridge) in the direction of Hastings, the photograph shows the goods yard and Kent & East Sussex Railway bay platform, the main South Eastern Railway station buildings being on the right of the picture. Note the lack of a run-round loop for KESR trains (this having to be done in the yard leading to the bay platform); also the large running-in board with 'CHANGE FOR KENT & EAST SUSSEX LINE'. *R. F. Roberts*

Below left:
One of the Class A1 'Terriers' — No 3 or No 5 — at Robertsbridge Junction after arriving with a train of ex-LSWR stock from Tenterden Town. *Author's collection*

Above right:
Class P No 1556, on hire from the Southern Railway, waits to leave Robertsbridge Junction with a train for Tenterden Town on 1 September 1938. *Roger Carpenter collection*

Centre right:
Lazy afternoon at Robertsbridge Junction *c*1936, with Class P 0-6-0T No 1325, on hire from the Southern Railway, coupled to an ex-LSWR bogie non-corridor Brake Third. Behind the tank engine is an ex-LNWR van now in LMS service. *C. Hamilton Ellis*

Below:
A postwar photograph, taken shortly after Nationalisation, showing Class A1X 'Terrier' No 2678, in black livery, on hire from the Southern, with a mixed train made up of a 1942-purchased ex-LSWR bogie corridor Composite (of which the company had two) and a string of wagons with an ex-LSWR road van at the rear. Waiting to shunt the yard, a Maunsell 2-6-0 stands in the down platform road, on the main line, normally used for London–Hastings trains. *Lens of Sutton collection*

Above:
The same 'Terrier', by now carrying its British Railways number (32678), departs Robertsbridge Junction with a single ex-LSWR bogie corridor Brake Composite and heads for Salehurst Halt on the first stage of its journey to Tenterden Town in June 1949. *Lens of Sutton collection*

Below:
No 32678 again, this time with a mixed train of ex-LSWR bogie corridor carriage and a rake of five- and eight-plank wagons between Hudson's Flour Mill and Robertsbridge Junction station. This is a train from Tenterden Town. The track on the near side is a long siding that leads from Robertsbridge to halfway to Hudson's Mill. *Lens of Sutton collection*

Hudson's Flour Mill

Above:
Class A1X 'Terrier' No 32655 (now preserved on the Bluebell Railway as *Stepney*) shunts Hudson's Flour Mill in the winter of 1951/2. Hudson's Mill was the only industrial premises served by the Kent & East Sussex Railway, apart from some Ministry of Supply Nissen huts at Tenterden Town station. Hudson's Mill was still rail served after 1961 from Robertsbridge goods yard, bulk grain traffic lasting until 1970, using privately owned Class P 0-6-0T No 31556, which is now preserved on the Kent & East Sussex Railway. *W. M. J. Jackson*

Below:
Hudson's Mill from the level crossing on 11 June 1961, the day before the line to Tenterden Town would close to all traffic. By now this was the only surviving traffic on the line. *Tom Middlemass*

Salehurst Halt

Above:
Salehurst Halt *c*1953, showing the rather basic timber and earth platform with no shelter and only a bare wooden bench for comfort. The halt served the nearby hamlet of Salehurst, comprising a church, a public house (now called the Salehurst Halt) and a cluster of houses. *Author's collection*

Left:
Class A1 0-6-0T No 3 arrives at Salehurst Halt *c*1936 with a train for Robertsbridge Junction. *Author's collection*

Junction Road Halt

Right:
'Terrier' No 32678 approaches Junction Road Halt with a mixed train for Tenterden in the winter of 1953/4. The train is passing the well-known hop fields of the Guinness brewery, which produced most of the hops for that firm's Park Royal Brewery in West London. The leading carriage is an ex-SECR 'Birdcage' brake, a common sight on the line in British Railways days. *Author's collection*

Below:
The second Junction Road Halt *c*1953. This structure was built in 1946 using concrete parts supplied by the Southern Railway from Exmouth concrete works near Exeter and replaced the original halt, of similar design and build to that at Salehurst. The platform was designed for a two-carriage train and served part of the Guinness hop farm.
The sign is a bit deceptive, however, as Hawkhurst is a good four miles away.
Author's collection

Bodiam

Above:
The way ahead near Bodiam on 26 April 1947, photographed from the open 'droplite' window of an ex-LSWR bogie non-corridor Brake Third heading towards Junction Road Halt from Bodiam station. A 'Terrier' and vintage bogie carriage in a truly rural scene that was to change in only a decade. *H. C. Casserley*

Below:
Hired 'Terrier' No 2678 shunts its train at Bodiam goods yard during its journey from Tenterden Town to Robertsbridge Junction *c*1947. Shunting mixed trains including passenger stock was a common practice in the company's independent days. *Lens of Sutton collection*

Above:
Bodiam station in the winter of 1953/4, only a few months before closure, with its corrugated-iron building from 1900, oil lamps on the platform and its blue enamel sign with white lettering. The siding on the left could be reached only from the easterly direction, as there was no run-round loop at this station. The station served Bodiam, with its famous castle, and Ewhurst village, up the hill from the station.

BODIAM TRACK PLAN

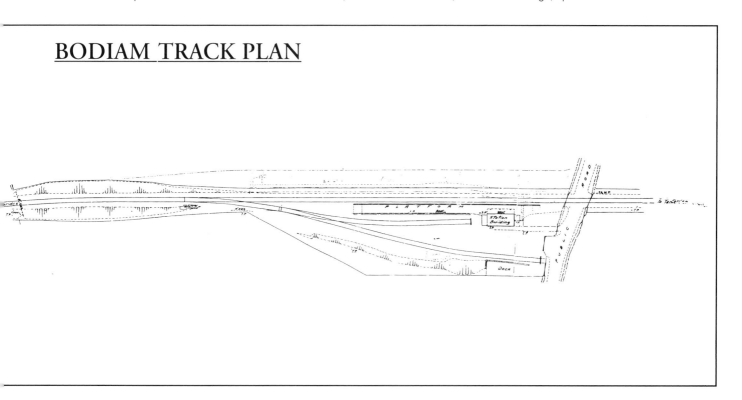

Above:
Bodiam station viewed from the level crossing towards Robertsbridge Junction on a winter's afternoon *c*1938. 'Terrier' No 2678, on hire from the Southern, simmers at the platform, awaiting the 'road' to Northiam with a single ex-LSWR bogie non-corridor Brake Third. *Author's collection*

Left:
An original Rother Valley lower-quadrant home signal stands sentinel on the approach to Bodiam from Northiam *c*1954. The station and the goods siding can be seen in the middle distance. *D. Lawrence*

Northiam

Right:
Northiam on 8 April 1955, a year and
four months after closure to passengers.
This photograph, taken in the direction of
Tenterden during the course of a Good Friday
walk along the line, shows the goods yard
with its two sidings and the long curved loop
running through the station platform. On the
far left can be seen the bank of earth that
was once the second platform, by this time
long disused and demolished. The catch
points in the foreground were installed during
the early days of British Railways; previously
there was nothing to prevent wagons' rolling
onto the main line. The large brick building in
the background is the warehouse of the
Southern Counties Agricultural Trading
Society (SCATS). *R. F. Roberts*

Above:
A 1930s photograph of Northiam, again taken
in the direction of Tenterden, showing both
platforms in use and the Rother Valley lower-
quadrant home signal in the middle distance.
This is a truly rustic scene, with corrugated-
iron station, oil lamps and basic wooden
benches in a run-down condition, while in the
background the trees form a natural arch
across the track. *H. C. Casserley*

Right:
We return to Good Friday (8 April) 1955,
about 20 years after the last picture was
taken. The station building basks in the mid-
day sunshine, awaiting long-lost passengers
that will never arrive or depart. Next to the
Gents' toilet (far left), the first door leads to
the parcels and goods office. The next door
on the right leads to the booking hall and
waiting room. *R. F. Roberts*

Left:
A rare photograph, taken on the same day as the previous picture, of the rear of Northiam station. This view in the direction of Tenterden Town shows the doors to the coal office (far right), the parcels office (centre) and the booking hall (left, with concrete steps leading up). *R. F. Roberts*

Below:
Northiam station viewed from the level crossing on 21 August 1949, towards Robertsbridge Junction. This picture shows the building from the other end, with the coal office and the Gents' toilet at the Tenterden end of the station. The ex-LSWR bogie Corridor Brake Composite stands at the single surviving platform, the 'Terrier' 0-6-0T having left to shunt the goods yard.
G. A. Hookham

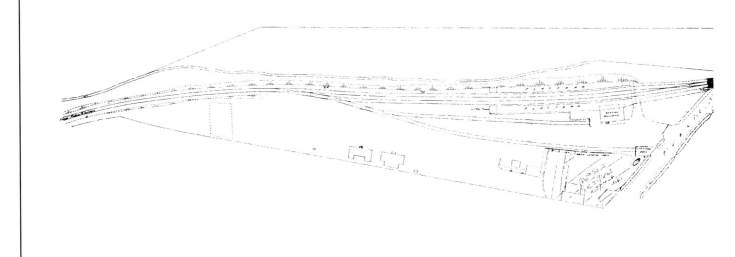

NORTHIAM TRACK PLAN *c*1930

NORTHIAM STATION BUILDING

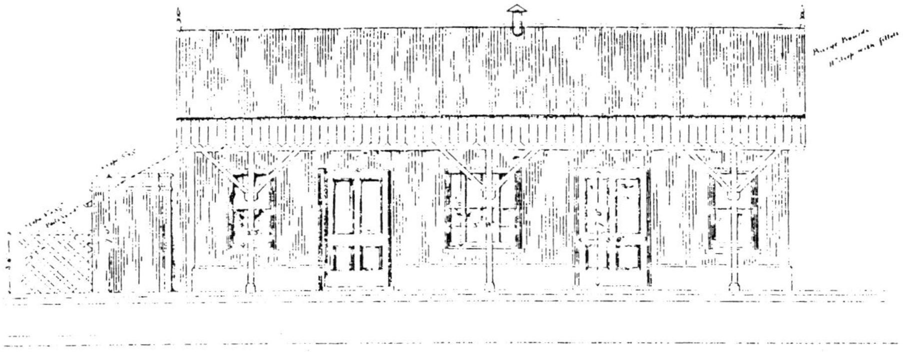

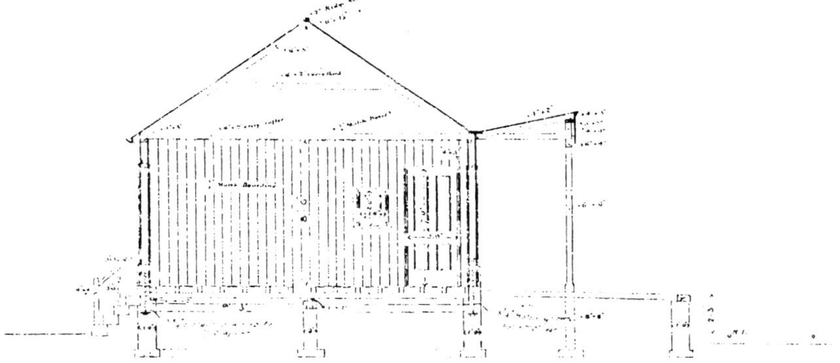

— Cross Section. —

— Elevation to Line. —

Goods Shed

Waiting Room

Booking Office

Store

Urinal

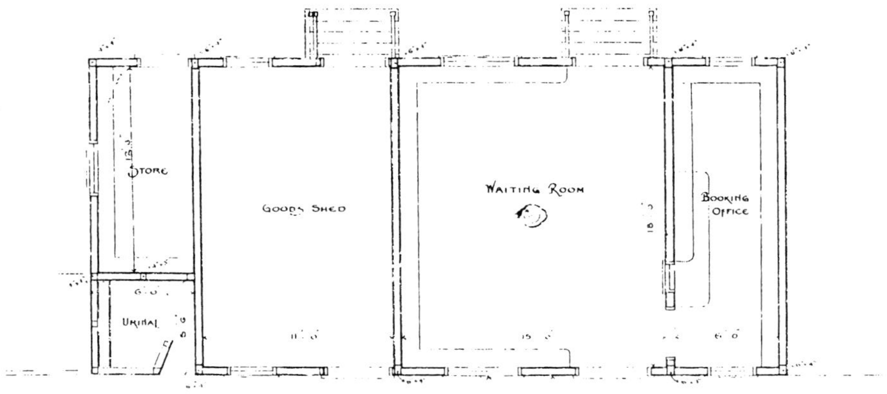

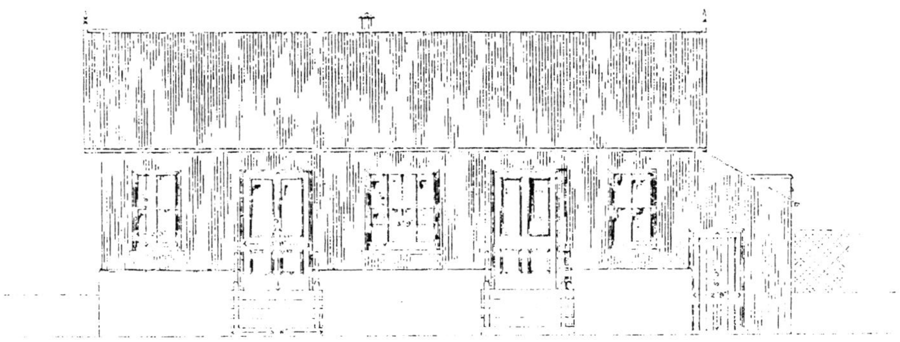

Rother Bridge

Above:
The Rother bridge viewed from the Robertsbridge side in early June 1961. This 66ft span was one of the most important structures on the line.
David Knapman

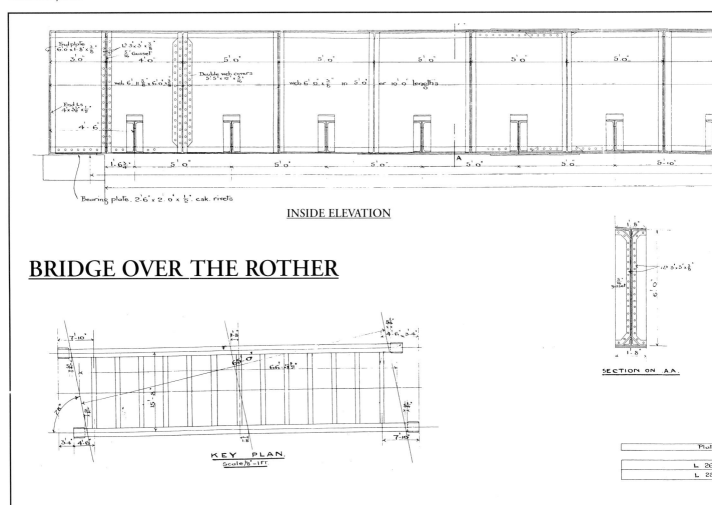

Above:
The same bridge from the opposite bank. The concrete blocks with slots at the far end are the remnants of a wartime anti-tank trap built in 1940 to prevent the advance of an invading army. Note also the pillbox on the far left. *David Knapman*

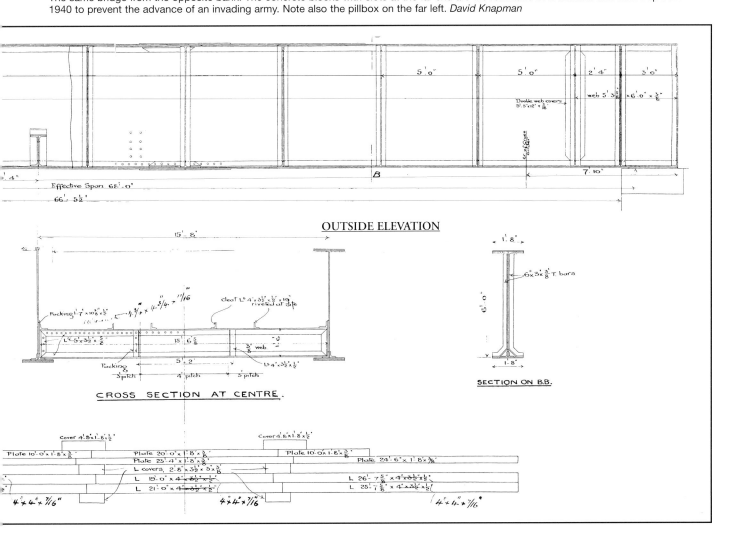

OUTSIDE ELEVATION

CROSS SECTION AT CENTRE.

SECTION ON B.B.

Wittersham Road

Above:
Class A1 'Terrier' 0-6-0T No 3 leaves
Wittersham Road station *c*1934 with a
single non-corridor ex-LSWR bogie Brake
Third and a single open wagon heading for
Robertsbridge Junction. At this point the line
climbs a steep bank to reach the Rother
Bridge, between Wittersham and Northiam
stations. *Author's collection*

Left:
A very bleak-looking Wittersham Road
station, photographed on Good Friday
(8 April) 1955, in the direction of Tenterden.
This building had no awning and — unlike all
the other Rother Valley stations — was built
at a right-angle to the platform. The layout of
the building was similar to that at Northiam,
with a coal office (far left), parcels room
(centre door) and booking hall (far right, next
to the platform and level crossing).
R. F. Roberts

Below left:
A further view of Wittersham Road station,
recorded on Monday 28 February 1955 and
showing the building from the northern end;
note (right) the steps up to the platform.
R. F. Roberts

Above right:
Wittersham Road station photographed in
the direction of Tenterden, June 1929,
showing the two-armed slotted signal with its
archaic spectacle plates and wooden lower
quadrant arms. Note the white circle (instead
of a white bar) — a feature abandoned by
most companies prior to World War 1. The
signals at this station and at High Halden
are believed to have been acquired second-hand
from the SER. *Author's collection*

WITTERSHAM ROAD TRACK PLAN *c*1930

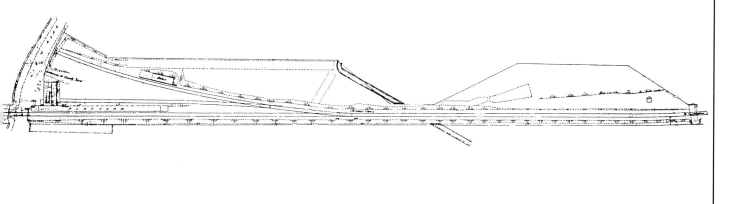

Rolvenden

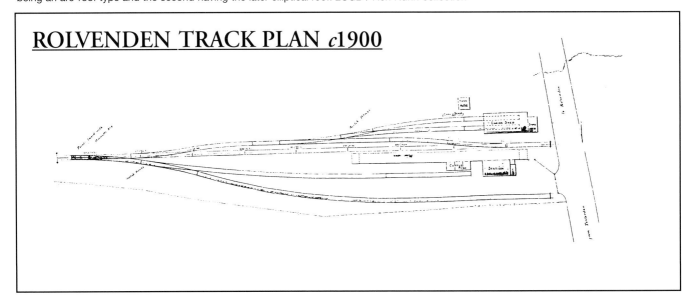

ROLVENDEN TRACK PLAN *c*1900

Above:
A view of the approach to Rolvenden yard and station on Monday 28 February 1955, showing the Rother Valley home signal from the other side. *R. F. Roberts*

ROLVENDEN TRACK PLAN *c*1930

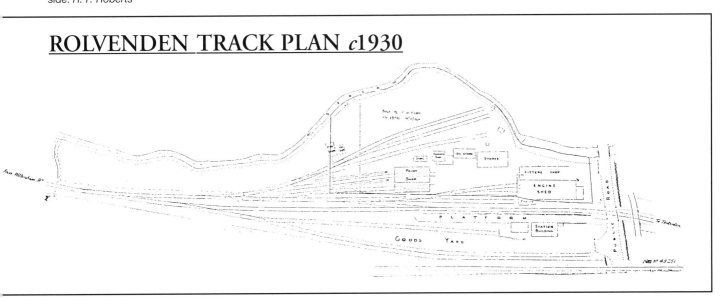

Above left:
A general view of Rolvenden station and shed *c*1934. When the line opened in 1900 this station was known as Tenterden, a horse bus providing a link to and from the town; in 1905, when the line was extended to Tenterden Town, it was renamed Rolvenden. Thereafter it saw few passengers and enjoyed a sleepy existence, with no permanent station staff. However, the locomotive depot/works was a very vibrant place and formed the hub of engineering activity on the line. Here 0-6-0ST No 8 *Hesperus* backs into the shed after its turn of duty. *Author's collection*

Left:
Rolvenden shed and works *c*1935, with the second No 4 (ex-LSWR 0-6-0ST No 0335), which, along with two spare boilers, had been acquired from the Southern Railway in 1932 in exchange for the first No 4, 0-8-0T *Hecate*. This was the second shed building, which replaced the original timber building, with curved roof, built in 1899. On the right can be seen the water tanks used to supply the works and replenish the locomotives; this would be replaced postwar by the present water tank in the yard. *Author's collection*

Above:
Ex-Great Western 0-6-0ST No 8 undergoing a heavy overhaul inside Rolvenden shed on 29 August 1925. The *Hesperus* nameplates would be removed in the early 1930s. *H. C. Casserley*

Right:
Inside Rolvenden shed *c*1930, with ex-LSWR 'Ilfracombe' goods 0-6-0 No 7 *Rother* (right) and ex-LBSCR Class A1 'Terrier' 0-6-0T No 5 *Rolvenden*, jacked up with its wheels removed during a heavy overhaul. This small works was the centre of engineering activity on the railway. This situation continued until the railway was nationalised in 1948, when Rolvenden became a subshed of Ashford. *LCGB / Ken Nunn collection*

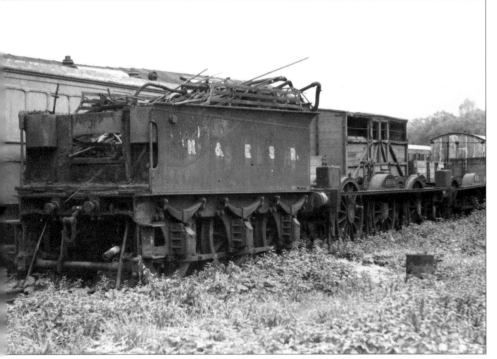

Above:
From the mid-1930s the Kent & East Sussex Railway was forced to hire locomotives from the Southern Railway, because its own aged fleet could no longer be relied upon. The hired types included ex SECR Class P 0-6-0Ts, ex-LBSCR Class A1X 'Terrier' 0-6-0Ts and ex-LSWR Class 0395 and SECR Class O1 0-6-0s. Here, on Saturday 26 March 1938, Class P No 1556 stands at the station platform at Rolvenden, awaiting the road to Robertsbridge Junction with a single ex-LSWR bogie Brake Third. *R. F. Roberts*

Below:
Following nationalisation in 1948 the line settled down to using 'Terriers' on the Rother Valley section and 'O1s' on the Headcorn extension. Seen *c*1953, an unidentified 'O1', with a single ex-LSWR bogie Corridor Brake Composite forming a train from Headcorn Junction, waits outside Rolvenden station; presently a member of staff will open the gates and set the signal to the 'off' position, whereupon the train will run into the station to complete its journey. Services to/from Headcorn and Robertsbridge were advertised as commencing from or terminating at Tenterden Town but also served Rolvenden, mostly unrecorded in the timetable. This part of the line, curving away towards Tenterden, was one of the author's favourites. *Author's Collection*

Above:
In the afternoon gloom 0-6-0T No 3 *Bodiam* and 0-6-0ST No 4 head out of Rolvenden towards Tenterden Town with a stock movement of a single ex-LSWR Brake Third bogie carriage. Train formations of this kind were occasionally carried out on the Rother Valley section as the bridges were designed to take light axle loadings and could not take double-headed trains. *C. Hamilton Ellis*

Below:
The approach to Rolvenden station, photographed in the direction of Robertsbridge Junction on Monday 28 February 1955, almost 14 months after the last passenger train ran and shortly before the demolition men moved in to flatten the shed and the station building. *R. F. Roberts*

Tenterden Town

Above:
'Terrier' No 3 arrives at Tenterden Town *c*1937 with a train from Robertsbridge Junction consisting of an ex-LSWR Panter arc-roofed Brake Third. *Author's collection*

Left:
The combination of 'Terrier' No 3 and a single ex-LSWR bogie carriage, about to depart as the 4.25pm to Robertsbridge Junction, viewed from the level crossing at Tenterden Town station on 22 July 1938. *R. F. Roberts*

Above:
A photograph of the new Tenterden Town station *c*1907, showing the platforms and goods yard full of rolling stock, including some of the bogie carriages rebuilt from four-wheeled vehicles and the new stock for the Headcorn extension. There is also evidence of a sizeable quantity of coal and cattle traffic. *Lens of Sutton collection*

TENTERDEN STATION BUILDING

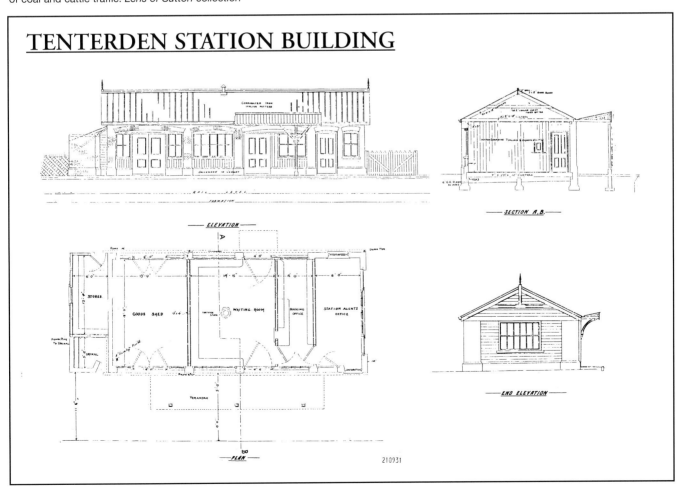

Left:
KESR No 4 (ex-SR No E0335) at Tenterden Town *c*1935 with a train for Robertsbridge Junction. The carriage formation is of interest, featuring an ex-GER four-wheel brake and the one-time LSWR Royal Saloon. Taken in the direction of Headcorn Junction, the photograph also shows the island platform and the wind pump used for pumping the water for the water tower and station.
Author's collection

Centre left:
A general view of Tenterden Town recorded on a quiet winter's afternoon in the early 1930s, showing the (then) gated crossing, three-arm signal and water tower. The lack of passengers helps to explain why the railway made so little money. *Author's collection*

Below left:
Photographed from the island platform, 2-4-0T No 2 *Northiam* arrives at Tenterden Town on 22 July 1938 with the 4.45pm mixed train from Robertsbridge Junction to Headcorn Junction, comprising an ex-LSWR arc-roof, non-corridor Brake Third and a rake of six- and eight-plank wagons. In the background (left) can be seen the ex-North London Railway passenger brake van shunted against the stock blocks.
R. F. Roberts

Above right:
Tenterden Town on 1 September 1938. Class A1 'Terrier' No 3 has just arrived with a train from Headcorn Junction, while the train on the right has arrived from Robertsbridge Junction behind hired Southern Class P No 1556 (out of camera shot). Both carriages are of ex-LSWR arc-roof non-corridor stock.
R. K. Cope

Centre right:
Ten years later, in the first summer of nationalisation, No 3 again heads a train from the island platform at Tenterden Town; by now the 'Terrier' has been rebuilt (at St Leonards shed in 1943) with a spare 'A1X' boiler from the Southern Railway. Note that the waste ground (left) has had wartime Nissen huts built upon it, while on the platform concrete electric lamps have replaced the earlier oil lamps. The carriages are both ex-LSWR bogie vehicles.
R. S. Carpenter collection

Right:
Class A1X 'Terrier' No 2640, on hire from the Southern, stands at the platform at Tenterden Town station *c*1947 with a train for Headcorn Junction as a passenger and two schoolboys chat to the driver. This locomotive had won its designer, William Stroudley, a gold medal for design at the Paris Exhibition of 1878.
Lens of Sutton collection

Above:
The view towards Headcorn Junction on 8 July 1939, as a solitary ex-LSWR bogie non-corridor Brake Third, awaiting a locomotive to work its next service, stands at the main platform at Tenterden Town.
R. F. Roberts

Left:
The ground-frame 'box at the north end of Tenterden Town station, photographed c1954.
R. Barnard

Left:
On a warm summer's afternoon in 1952 an unidentified 'O1' 0-6-0 heads out of Tenterden Town towards Headcorn Junction with a single ex-LSWR bogie corridor Brake Composite. In the background can be seen the tall double-armed home signal which controlled both platforms at the station.
Author's collection

Top:
Class O1 0-6-0 No 31065 shunts 16-ton mineral wagons in the coal sidings at Tenterden Town goods yard *c*1953. *Photos from the Fifties*

Above:
No 31065 makes up a train of opens in the sidings serving the MoS Nissen huts. Note the wooden-posted lower-quadrant home signal controlling the line to Headcorn Junction. *Photos from the Fifties*

Right:
The three-arm signal at Tenterden Town station that controlled the loop and the line to Rolvenden. *R. Barnard / Photos from the Fifties*

St Michael's Halt

Above:
A bit more welcoming than the halts near Robertsbridge (but not much), St Michael's Halt served the outskirts of Tenterden to the north of the Town station. This view towards Tenterden Town was recorded in the 1920s from the level crossing. The corrugated-iron hut served as a ticket office.
Author's collection

Left:
St Michael's Halt again, on 21 August 1938. The halt has now become very run-down, and the track weed-strewn. The ticket office is now closed, passengers having to purchase their tickets on the train.
Roger Carpenter collection

Below:
St Michael's Halt, Tenterden, c1953, photographed in the direction of Headcorn Junction. Note the poor condition of the platform. *Lens of Sutton collection*

St Michael's Tunnel

Above:
The south portal of St Michael's Tunnel, photographed on 30 August 1931. The tunnel was one of the line's main civil-engineering features, the others being the two large bridges on the Rother Valley section.
Author's collection

Right:
St Michael's Tunnel again, this time viewed from the north, towards St Michael's Halt and Tenterden Town, on 31 August 1938.
Roger Carpenter

High Halden Road

Left:
No 8, formerly *Hesperus*, heads a mixed train near High Halden Road *c*1935. Note the Rolvenden-designed coal bunker. 'Terrier' No 3 was also rebuilt with (and retains) this design of bunker. *Lens of Sutton collection*

Below left:
High Halden station *c*1950, photographed in the direction of Headcorn Junction. The timber-built station was similar in design to those on the Rother Valley section. Note the double-arm ex-SER signal and the awning, with its supports painted white to prevent passengers from walking into them during the wartime blackout. The goods yard was at the rear of the station. *Author's collection*

Right:
The double bi-directional home signal at High Halden, photographed in August 1951. *F. Hornby*

Below:
The view towards Tenterden Town from the platform at High Halden Road station on 30 April 1938. The line was very straight along this section. *Roger Carpenter collection*

HIGH HALDEN ROAD STATION BUILDING

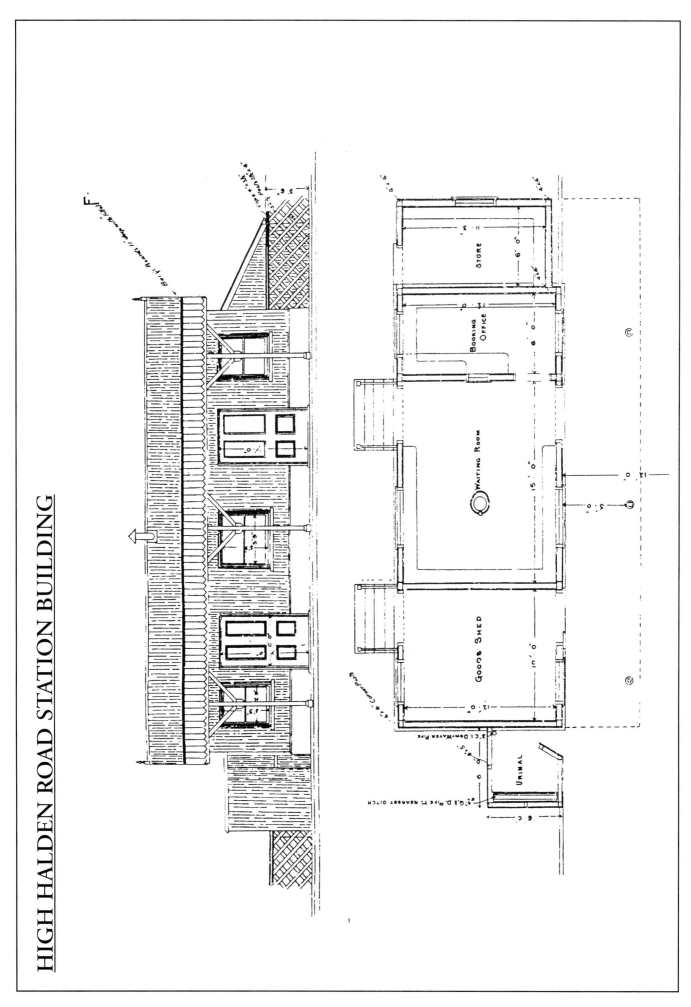

HIGH HALDEN ROAD TRACK PLAN

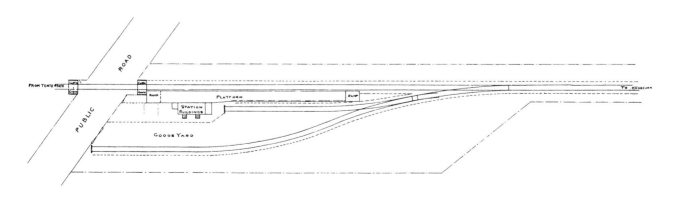

Biddenden

Above:
Class O1 0-6-0 No 31065 leaving Biddenden with the 10.55 Headcorn–Tenterden Town on 17 August 1953, four months before complete closure of this section of the line. *N. R. Knight*

Below:
A photograph taken at Biddenden station *c*1910, not long after the opening of the line from Tenterden Town to Headcorn Junction, showing the two platforms with the passing-loop and the fenced path from the road to the timber station. This was the view towards Headcorn Junction. Again, the two-siding goods yard could be found at the rear of the station. *Author's collection*

Above:
The view towards Tenterden Town at Biddenden on 30 August 1938. The station building is clearly well-maintained, having recently received a fresh coat of paint, while the permanent way is weed-free and well-ballasted. The corrugated-iron building on the far right is the station agent's bungalow — a feature at most of these stations. Note the home signal in the middle distance. *R. S. Carpenter collection*

Below:
Biddenden station building photographed on the same day from the opposite platform, with the station agent and a local boy standing in the doorway of the booking hall. The other open doorway is to the parcel and goods store. *Roger Carpenter collection*

BIDDENDEN STATION BUILDING

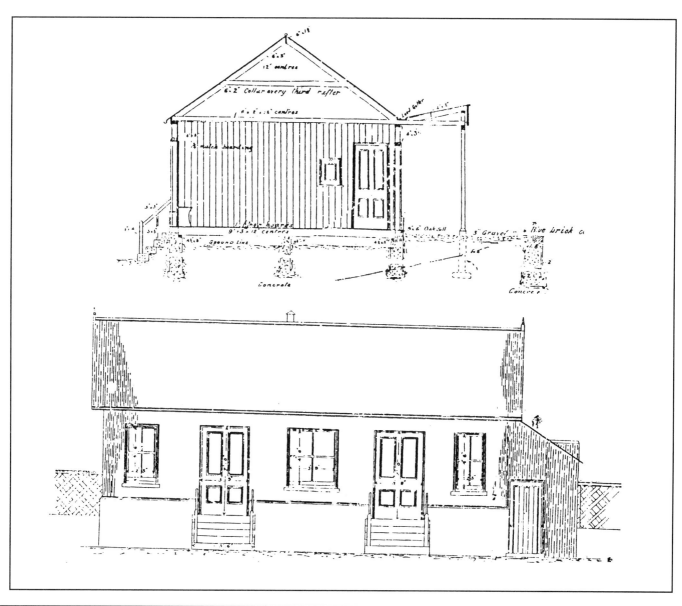

BIDDENDEN TRACK PLAN

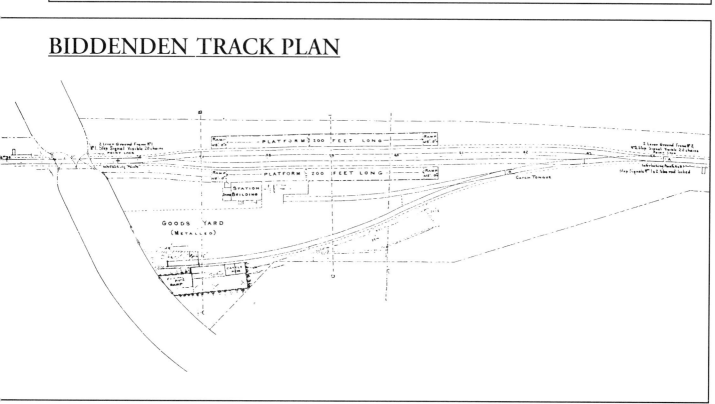

Frittenden Road

Above:
Frittenden Road station *c*1935, photographed in the direction of Headcorn Junction. The station building is similar to those at High Halden Road and Biddenden, but the timber-built platform makes quite a contrast with the brick-built structures at those locations. Note the signal, its arms attached to a single post. *Lens of Sutton collection*

Left:
Frittenden Road on 30 August 1938, photographed in the direction of Tenterden Town. Compared with Biddenden, the platform and station are in a run-down state. The signals are set for two trains running in opposite directions; was Will Hay the station agent? *Roger Carpenter collection*

Left:
Not long before closure, *c*1953, Frittenden Road station has taken on a neater look. Note that the signal has disappeared and that concrete fencing and sleepers are in evidence. The lady in tartan skirt and fur jacket looks hopeful for a train towards Headcorn Junction. *Lens of Sutton collection*

FRITTENDEN ROAD STATION BUILDING

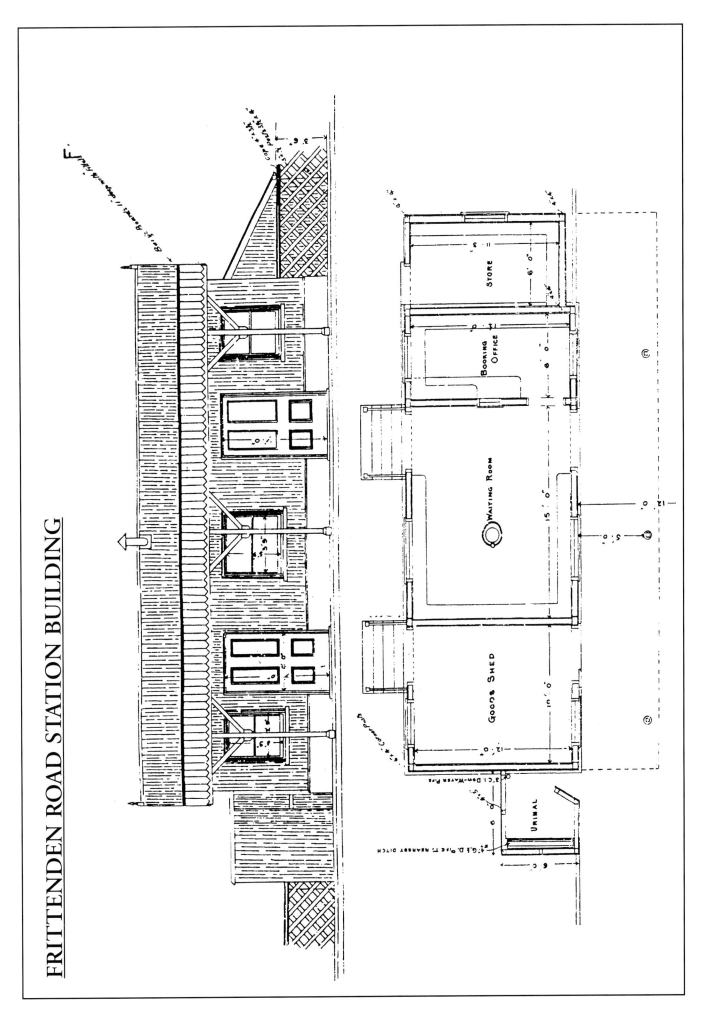

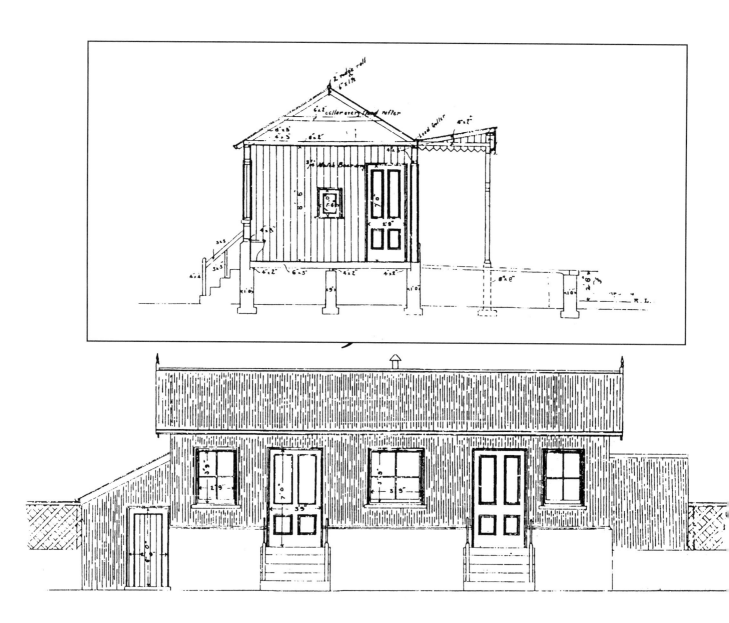

FRITTENDEN ROAD TRACK PLAN

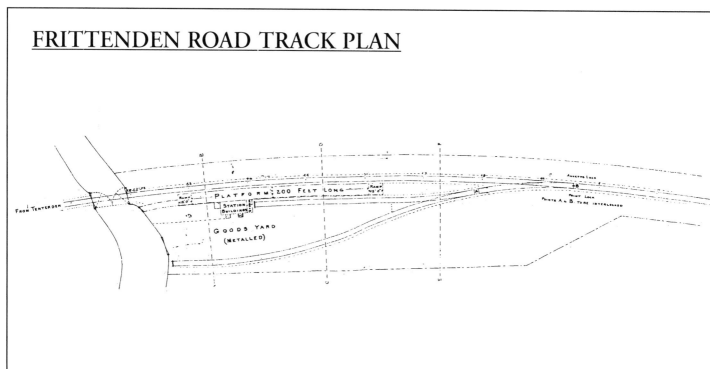

Headcorn Junction

Above:
The first Headcorn Junction station *c*1910, with a train of four- and six-wheel carriages at the platform. The corrugated-iron building was originally at Tenterden Town and was moved when the later brick building was constructed at that location. The timber-framed building in the background (behind the KESR station) is part of the SECR station on the London–Dover main line. *Author's collection*

Below:
Headcorn Junction station was remodelled in the early 1930s, with a concrete platform facing on a curved alignment. This was the view towards London on 30 August 1938, showing the yard with its extensive sidings and the exchange sidings beyond, past the West signalbox on the main line. *R. S. Carpenter collection*

59

Above:
The view towards Tenterden Town from Headcorn Junction in July 1937, showing well the platform's curvature and, in the distance, the Southern Railway-built home starter signal. *R. F. Roberts*

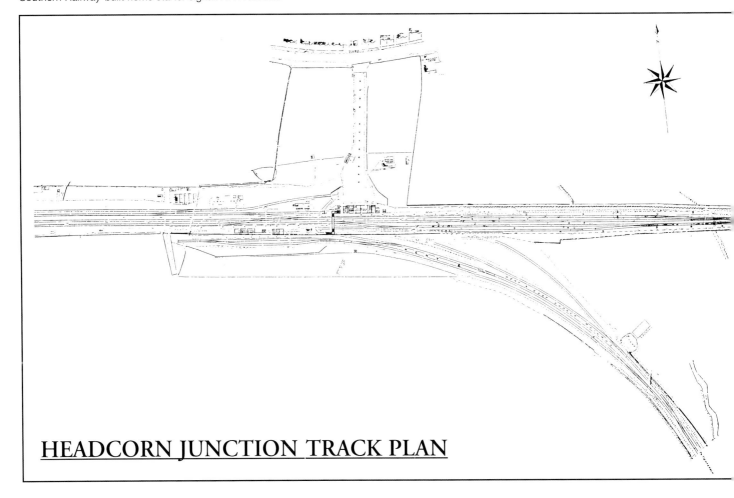

HEADCORN JUNCTION TRACK PLAN

Above:
Class P 0-6-0T No 1555 at Headcorn Junction with a train for Tenterden Town and Rolvenden *circa* June 1948, in the early months of state ownership. This was the last summer when one could see an old-style Kent & East Sussex train and ride on the railway in the traditional way; the Class P tanks would soon be replaced by Class O1 0-6-0 tender engines and Brighton Class A1X 'Terrier' 0-6-0Ts brought in to standardise motive power. *The Rev A. W. Mace*

Below:
Pictured at Headcorn Junction, with the main-line station and the footbridge in the background, 2-4-0T No 2 *Northiam* stands at the head of the 12.40pm mixed train to Tenterden Town and Rolvenden on Saturday 26 March 1938. The leading carriage is an ex-LSWR Third. *R. F. Roberts*

Motive Power

Left:
No 1 *Tenterden*, built by Hawthorne Leslie in 1899, in original condition at Rolvenden shed *c*1908. This shows the locomotive as built, with smaller wheels and copper-capped chimney and dome, in Rother Valley livery. In front of the locomotive can be seen the tender of No 7 *Rother*, one of the two ex-LSWR 'Ilfracombe' goods locomotives. *Author's collection*

Below left:
Another view of No 1 *Tenterden*, again at Rolvenden shed, this time in the early 1930s. The photograph shows the large wheels, fitted a few years after its delivery to the line, and the stovepipe chimney, fitted to both 2-4-0T locomotives. No 1 would be withdrawn from service in the mid-1930s and stored at Rolvenden, finally being cut up as part of the scrap drive of 1941.
H. C. Casserley

Top right:
No 2 *Northiam*, also built in 1899 by Hawthorne Leslie for the opening in April 1900 of the Rother Valley Railway, on which it hauled the first train. This attractive portrait shows the locomotive in clean lined Oxford blue, with garter motif and yellow straw lettering, at Rolvenden shed *c*1932. *Author's collection*

Above:
Never rebuilt with larger wheels, No 2 is pictured still in lined Oxford blue at Headcorn Junction station on Saturday 26 March 1938.
R. F. Roberts

Right:
No 2 *Northiam* arrives at Tenterden Town station with the 3.50pm from Robertsbridge to Headcorn on 26 March 1938. This machine was quite widely travelled, having been hired to the East Kent Railway in the early 1920s, the Weston, Clevedon & Portishead Light Railway later in the 1920s and finally in 1937 to Gainsborough Pictures for the filming of *Oh Mr Porter* on location at the abandoned (and by then half-lifted) Basingstoke & Alton Light Railway. Like its twin, it would be cut up during the scrap drive of 1941. *R. F. Roberts*

Above:
'Terrier' 0-6-0T No 3 *Bodiam* (ex-LBSCR No 70, built 1872) and 0-8-0T No 4 *Hecate* (Hawthorne Leslie, 1904) at Rolvenden shed yard *c*1905. The photograph shows No 3, purchased in 1901 by the Rother Valley Railway, in the condition in which it arrived, with condenser pipes and name painted onto the side tanks, before cast plates were fitted. Both locomotives are in lined Oxford-blue livery. *Author's collection*

Below:
No 3, still in A1 condition, at Headcorn Junction on Saturday 8 July 1939, about to depart with the 12.35pm train for Tenterden Town and Rolvenden. The condensing pipes have long since been removed, together with the nameplates. Livery is now a lined apple green, but throughout the changes the locomotive has retained its Stroudley copper-capped chimney. The non-corridor carriage is an ex-LSWR bogie Composite. Note the KESR ground-frame signalbox at the front of the locomotive. *R. F. Roberts*

Above:
'Terrier' among the Bulleids. No 3 in rebuilt 'A1X' form in the shed yard at Brighton after a heavy overhaul in 1947. By this time the locomotive had been repainted in Bulleid malachite green, lined in black and yellow, with shaded arched lettering. It had been rebuilt with an 'A1X' boiler at St Leonards shed in 1943, when the original needed replacement. *Author's collection*

Below:
No 3 has its smokebox cleaned out at Rolvenden shed *c*1947. The paintwork appears to be less well kept than in the previous photograph. *Author's collection*

Above:
A works official photograph of No 4 *Hecate* used by the Colonel as an official postcard to send short messages from his office at Tonbridge, Kent. *Author's collection*

Below:
Hawthorne Leslie 0-8-0T No 4 *Hecate*, at Rolvenden shed shortly after delivery in 1904. This handsome large tank was built for the proposed Maidstone extension, which, although authorised with a Parliamentary Act, was never constructed. The line would have connected Headcorn with Maidstone via Sutton Valance; at the time it was envisaged that there would be a large volume of freight traffic from North Kent, but this was not to be. *Author's collection*

Right:
A photograph of No 4 *Hecate* at Rolvenden in the mid-1920s, taken from the right-hand side and showing the later, more austere Kent & East Sussex Railway lettering and plain blue livery. The locomotive was steamed on average once a week to keep it in good order. Owing to its weight it could work only between Rolvenden and Headcorn Junction. *Author's collection*

Centre right:
A rare photograph of No 4 in store at Rolvenden with No 7 *Rother c*1929. Apart from its weekly outing to Headcorn, it was used during Biddenden Fair week, when there was plenty of cattle traffic. During World War 1 the locomotive had been loaned to the East Kent Railway. *Author's collection*

Below:
Colonel Stephens died in October 1931, after which W. H. Austen, his loyal assistant, started to make economies that were hitherto unthinkable. The Colonel had had a soft spot for *Hecate* and probably dreamed that one day his 0-8-0T would work heavy trains up Sutton Valance Hill on the proposed Maidstone extension, but it was not to be: in 1932 Austen exchanged it with the Southern Railway for an ex-LSWR '0330' saddle tank (SR No E0335) and two spare boilers. Following overhaul *Hecate* re-entered service as SR No 949 and thereafter spent most of its working life based at Nine Elms shed in London, where it is seen *c*1936. Used on carriage-shunting duties at Clapham Junction until withdrawal in 1950, it was latterly fitted with a Brighton boiler, which rendered it a lot less handsome. *Lens of Sutton collection*

Above:
The second No 4 (ex SR No E0335) at Rolvenden shortly after arriving on the line *c*1933. The East Kent Railway had purchased sister No 0127 in December 1925, and it was the loan of this locomotive *en route* to its new owner that prompted the KESR's acquisition of No E0335 in exchange for *Hecate*. Upon arrival the new No 4 had a Beyer Peacock Beattie-type boiler, but this would subsequently be replaced by a Drummond-type boiler. *Lens of Sutton collection*

Below:
No 4, by now with Drummond boiler, at Headcorn in the summer of 1948 following withdrawal from service. It had been hauled here from Rolvenden in the spring, shortly after British Railways took over, along with the line's remaining four-wheel carriages, which were then broken up. No 4 would later be towed to Ashford Works, where it too was scrapped. *Author's collection*

Above:
Formerly LBSCR No 71 *Wapping*, Class A1 'Terrier' 0-6-0T No 5 *Rolvenden*, built 1872, stands at Rolvenden yard (Tenterden station) just after arriving on the line in 1905, painted in lined Oxford blue. It was to lead a less eventful life than No 3 *Bodiam*, being withdrawn in the early 1930s and contributing parts for the latter's rebuilding later in the decade. *Author's collection*

Below:
No 5 *Rolvenden*, again at Rolvenden, this time *c*1925 and apparently in unlined blue, with one of the 2-4-0Ts in the background. Both 'Terriers' retained their Stroudley copper-capped chimneys. *Lens of Sutton collection*

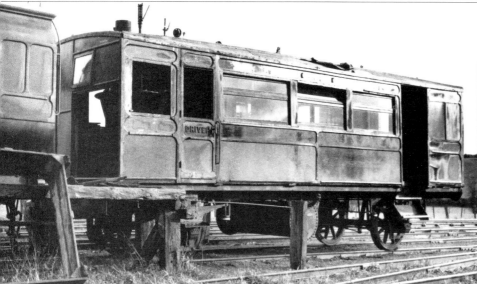

Above:
The R. Y. Pickering steam railcar — No 6 in the locomotive register and No 16 in the carriage register — at the Pickering works *c*1906. It ran for a number of years, off and on, until the outbreak of World War 1 in August 1914, after which it was stored out of use at Rolvenden yard. *Author's collection*

Left:
Run-down and forlorn in the carriage siding at Rolvenden *c*1935, No 16 — as it was by then — stands with flaking paintwork and missing body panels. The upright boiler is just discernible on the left, through the open panels of the coal-storage area.
Roger Carpenter collection

Below:
A clearer view of the boiler at Rolvenden *c*1936. The railcar would be broken up in 1941, but its underframe still exists as part of the water tower at Rolvenden.
C. Hamilton Ellis

Above:
The Colonel had a liking for certain classes of locomotive that seemed to be successful when put to work on light railways. In this respect the Brighton A1 'Terrier' was closely followed by the LSWR 'Ilfracombe' goods 0-6-0, of which the KESR had two. Recently delivered No 7 *Rother* (ex LSWR No 0349), running as an 0-4-2, is seen at Rolvenden *c*1910 in lined Oxford-blue livery with polished brass dome. *Author's collection*

Right:
Rother awaiting its next turn of duty at Rolvenden shed, 29 August 1925.
H. C. Casserley

Below:
No 7 *Rother* in later light-railway life, in less attractive condition only a year or so from being laid up at Rolvenden. This photograph, taken *c*1930, shows the locomotive in unlined Oxford blue in the storage siding at Rolvenden. The two 'Ilfracombe' goods locomotives gave good service to the KESR and were totally worn out by the time of their withdrawal in the early 1930s. *Lens of Sutton collection*

Above:
0-6-0ST No 8 was purchased in 1914 from the Bute Supply Co. Built in 1876 by Manning, Wardle & Co of Leeds, it was originally named *Ringing Rock* and was numbered 1380 by the Great Western Railway, which had acquired the locomotive along with the North Pembrokeshire & Fishguard Railway in 1898. It is seen here in store at Rolvenden in the summer of 1936. *C. Hamilton Ellis*

Left:
A profile of No 8 at Rolvenden *c*1936, showing to advantage the attractive lines of this delightful locomotive. *Jim Jarvis*

Left:
No 8 again, in store at Rolvenden shed on 26 March 1938. When acquired by the KESR it still bore the name *Ringing Rock*, which was removed shortly after its arrival, the plates going onto a Manning Wardle 0-6-0ST on the Selsey Tramway. No 8 was renamed *Hesperus*, which would appear to have brought it mixed fortunes: in 1918 it was involved in an accident, becoming derailed between Northiam and Bodiam after floodwater had washed away the line. After the accident No 8 lost its *Hesperus* plates, thereafter remaining nameless. It was withdrawn in 1940 and cut up as part of the wartime scrap drive. *R. F. Roberts*

Above:
Rebuilt 'Ilfracombe' goods 0-6-0 No 9 *Juno* (ex LSWR No 0284), built 1873 and acquired by the KESR in 1914, stands on shed at Rolvenden in the mid-1920s. The two 'Ilfracombes' represented a good investment for the line, working heavy trains for more than 20 years. *Author's collection*

Below:
No 9 *Juno* towards the end of its life, at Rolvenden shed *c*1930, in company with Hawthorn Leslie 2-4-0T No 1 *Tenterden*, also by now on its last legs. Nos 7 and 9 would both spend many years in the dump at Rolvenden before being cut up during the scrap drive of 1941. *Lens of Sutton collection*

Above:
Transition at Rolvenden: the first Model T Ford railbus set shortly after its arrival in 1923. The three petrol railbus sets delivered to the Kent & East Sussex Railway — two Fords and one Shefflex — represented an attempt to cut running costs, made necessary by a drop in receipts after World War 1. *Lens of Sutton collection*

Below:
The first Ford Model T set at Rolvenden yard in the summer of 1930. These sets were a brave attempt to keep the railway going at a time of depression and cutbacks. The Colonel purchased petrol rail cars for most of his standard-gauge lines except the East Kent Railway.
H. C. Casserley

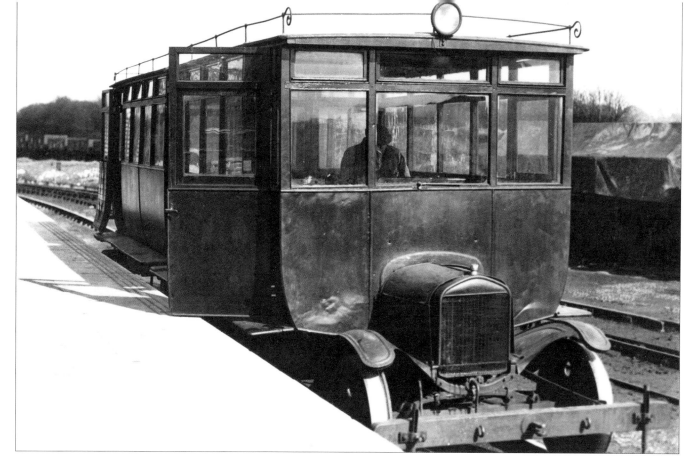

Above:
The same set at Robertsbridge Junction on 14 March 1931. The railbus sets were not very comfortable vehicles in which to ride, and the all-pervading smell of petrol was enough to put anyone off travelling on the line for evermore. *R. S. Carpenter collection*

Below:
Delivered in 1924, the second Ford railbus set was rarely photographed but is seen here arriving at Rolvenden with a service from Robertsbridge Junction *c*1932. All three of the KESR's railbus sets were two-car units, but a three-car set ran for a time on the Shropshire & Montgomeryshire Light Railway. *Lens of Sutton collection*

Above:
In 1929 the Colonel ordered a two-car petrol railbus set from Shefflex Motors of Sheffield. This was more substantial than the Ford sets, with heavier chassis and bodywork; it is seen in the early 1930s on a service from Robertsbridge Junction. Note the luggage trolley, a feature of these railbus sets. *R. S. Carpenter collection*

Below:
Shefflex railbus set No 3 at Rolvenden yard c1934, with luggage trolley at rear. *H. C. Casserley*

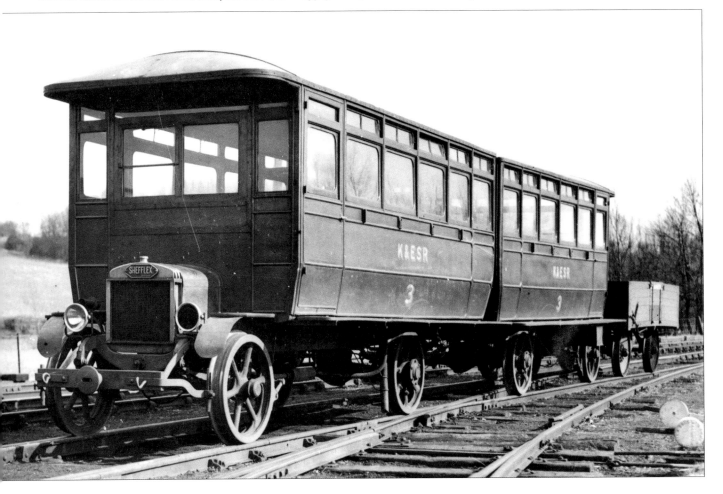

Above:
The Shefflex set at Rolvenden on 5 May 1935. The arrival of the three railbus sets heralded the withdrawal of a number of the longstanding steam locomotives and a quantity of older carriage stock.
J. H. L. Adams

Right:
The Shefflex set in store in the lean-to shed at Rolvenden c1934. *R. S. Carpenter collection*

Below:
The end of the railbus sets. Shefflex set No 3 and the first Ford set await the end at Rolvenden yard, 1939. *Lens of Sutton collection*

Carriage stock

Left:
All-Third No 2, one of the first six four-wheel carriages purchased by the Rother Valley Railway, from Hurst Nelson in 1900.
Nos 1-4 were all-Third vehicles seating 32 passengers, Nos 5 and 6 being all-First vehicles seating 28 in two inter-connected compartments, to separate smoking from non-smoking passengers. *Author's collection*

Left:
An official photograph of RVR carriage No 5 showing to good effect the vehicle's fine lines and the detail of the running-gear and panelwork. *Author's collection*

Below:
Hawthorn Leslie 2-4-0T No 1 *Tenterden*, in original condition with small driving wheels, stands at Northiam *c*1901 with a train of original RVR four-wheelers and the two newly acquired ex-Great Eastern Railway four-wheeled brake vehicles. In 1910 No 9, with two compartments, was stripped out to provide a full brake vehicle, while No 10, which had three compartments, had seats removed to provide a gangway on one side; the latter vehicle was later sold to the Shropshire & Montgomeryshire Railway, where it lasted until 1952. *A. Vaughan collection*

Above:
In 1904 the six four-wheel carriages were sent to R. Y. Pickering for rebuilding as bogie vehicles. They reappeared as three bogie carriages: a Brake Third (No 1) seating 48, a Brake Composite (No 4) seating 16 First- and 28 Third-class passengers and an all-Third (No 6) seating 64. Brake Third No 1 is seen at the R. Y. Pickering works as newly turned out. *HMRS collection*

Below:
All-Third No 6 in ex-works condition. These carriages were to see very little work following their return to the KESR, spending most of their lives stored in sidings at Rolvenden and at Tenterden before being broken up during the 1930s. *HMRS collection*

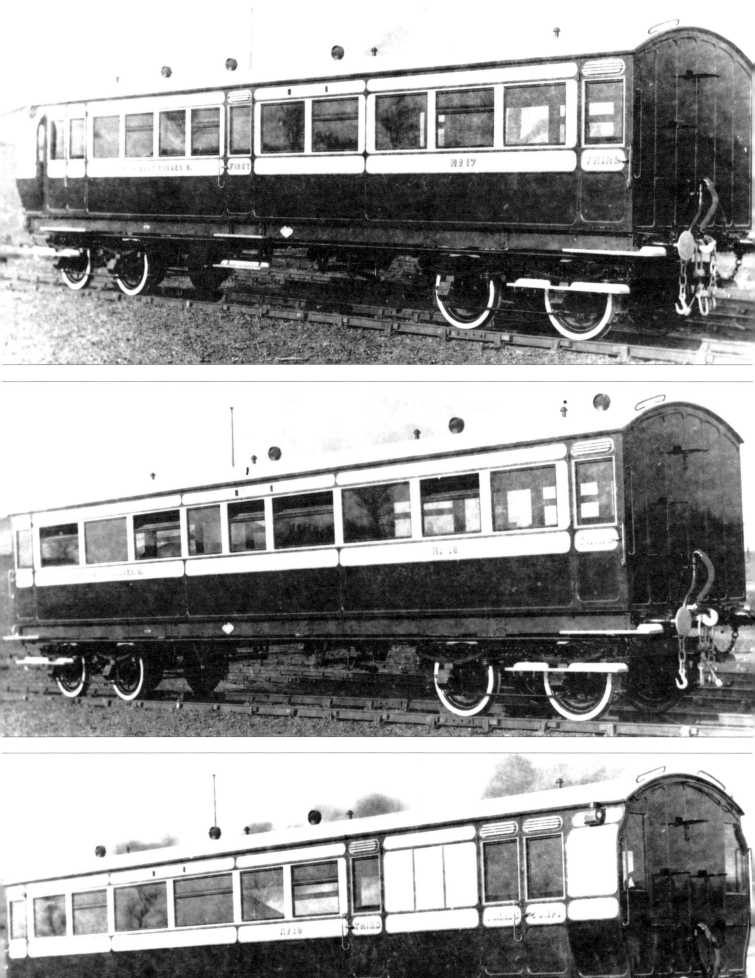

Left:
In 1905 the KESR acquired a new set of three bogie carriages constructed by R. Y. Pickering. Seen at the builder's works, No 17 was a Brake Composite seating 16 First- and 30 Third-class passengers in smoking and non-smoking sections. *HMRS collection*

Below left:
No 18 was a Third-class smoking/non-smoking carriage seating 48 passengers. When built these carriages were painted in a livery of light cream and medium chocolate brown, with white roof and black running gear. Wheel tyres were painted white. *HMRS collection*

Bottom left:
The third vehicle in the set was No 19, a smoking/non-smoking Brake Third seating 32. This photograph shows the brake compartment with its duckets. Note the grab-chains in addition to the screw couplings on the buffer-beam, an arrangement that also applied to the set of rebuilt four-wheel stock. *HMRS collection*

Above:
Carriage No 10 was none other than the one-time LSWR Royal Saloon of 1851, which when built had been exhibited at the Great Exhibition in Hyde Park. Together with a second four-wheeled Royal carriage of a different body design, built 1844, it was purchased from the LSWR in 1908 by the Plymouth, Devonport & South Western Junction Railway, from which both were later acquired by Colonel Stephens, for use on the Kent & East Sussex Railway and the Shropshire & Montgomeryshire Light Railway. What was to become No 10 arrived on the KESR c1909, although it was not numbered until another carriage bearing that number had been sold. Used at first as an inspection saloon, after numbering it became a First-class vehicle, being seen thus at Rolvenden yard c1935. *C. Hamilton Ellis*

Left:
A rare view of the inside of the Royal Saloon c1935, showing the grey upholstered settees and the rich walnut-panelled interior. No 10 had two compartments; this photograph is taken from the larger compartment, looking into the smaller seating area. *C. Hamilton Ellis*

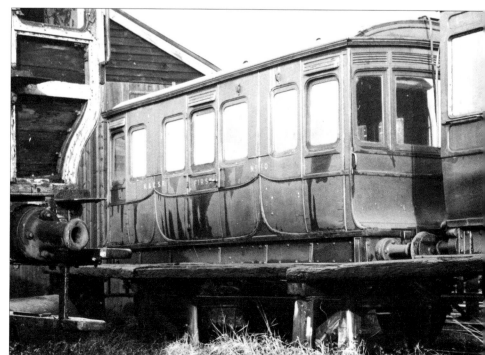

Right:
No 10 at Rolvenden c1936, shortly before its sale to the Southern Railway, which had intended to preserve the carriage as part of its proposed Eastleigh Museum project. However, during World War 2 the vehicle was broken up for scrap and its body sold for use as a summerhouse at Plaistow, Sussex, where it was finally destroyed in the early 1960s. *Author's collection*

Top:
Ex-LSWR four-wheel all-Third No 19 in store at Rolvenden yard, 26 March 1938. Seating 30 passengers, this was the second No 19, purchased in 1910 along with a second three-compartment all-Third. No 19 was to survive until 1948, when it was broken up at Headcorn. *R. F. Roberts*

Above:
Ex-LSWR Brake Third No 1 sandwiched between the two rail-mounted cranes at Rolvenden yard *c*1935. This carriage was purchased in 1911 and was described as duplicate stock, as at that time the number 1 was still held by the bogie-carriage rebuild of 1904. This vehicle lasted until 1948. *C. Hamilton Ellis*

Left:
Ex-LSWR six-wheel Composite No 4 coupled to No 19 in the goods yard at Rolvenden on 22 July 1938. This carriage was purchased in 1911 along with two four-wheel Brake Thirds. *R. F. Roberts*

Above:
An interesting line-up of carriage stock at Rolvenden *c*1935, featuring the ex-LSWR six-wheel Composite, recently repainted and as yet unlettered, behind which are an ex-Great Eastern Railway four-wheel brake and, furthest from the camera, a non-corridor ex-LSWR bogie brake vehicle. The lady by the first compartment door is Mrs Hamilton Ellis. *C. Hamilton Ellis*

Below:
Ex-LSWR Panter arc-roof bogie Brake Third No 2, seen at Rolvenden yard on 14 August 1937. The third KESR carriage so numbered, it had been obtained from the Southern Railway (2640) in exchange for derelict stock in 1932, when No 4 *Hecate* was exchanged for SR 0-6-0ST No E0335 and two spare boilers. Surprisingly the SR also accepted some derelict carriages in exchange for old but sound bogie stock. *H. C. Casserley*

Left:
Ex-LSWR non-corridor Composite No 5, acquired from the Southern Railway (2684) in 1936, in need of a repaint at Rolvenden yard *c*1946. This vehicle lasted in service until 1948. *Lens of Sutton collection*

Left:
The last carriages obtained for the KESR, in December 1943, were two LSWR bogie corridor brake vehicles (ex-Southern Nos 3093 and 3121), numbered 1 and 6 in the carriage list. Both lasted into British Railways days but were labelled for use only on the Kent & East Sussex line. No 6 is seen at Northiam in the summer of 1949 on a train for Tenterden Town. *Lens of Sutton collection*

Below:
Most of the vintage carriage stock was withdrawn after BR had taken over. Here a line of ex-LSWR vintage stock await breaking-up at Headcorn Junction in the summer of 1948. On the left can be seen 0-6-0ST No 4, also awaiting disposal. *Milepost 92½ / A.W. Mace collection*

Passenger-train formations

Above:
No 9 *Juno* stands at the original Headcorn Junction station in May 1930 with a mixed train of ex-LSWR carriage stock comprising two four-wheel brake vehicles either side of a six-wheeler. *Lens of Sutton collection*

Below:
In 1948, demonstrating the change in train formations in the intervening 18 years, 'O1' 0-6-0 No 1434, on hire from the SR, pauses at Headcorn Junction with one of the bogie corridor ex-LSWR carriages (No 1 or No 6). *T. J. Edgington*

Brake vans

Above:
An official photograph, taken at the R. Y. Pickering works in 1900, of one of two passenger brake vans supplied for the opening in April 1900. No 7 was later sold to the Selsey Tramway, while No 8 survived until 1935 on the Kent & East Sussex Railway. *HMRS collection*

Below:
Ex-North London Railway passenger brake van No 15 at Tenterden Town station on 27 March 1937. The company purchased two of these vehicles, numbered 14 and 15, in the early 1900s. No 14 was later sold to the East Kent Railway, No 15 remaining on the KESR until 1948. *Tom Middlemass collection*

Above:
The ex-Great Western brake van built in 1877. Purchased in 1905, it became No 24 in the KESR list and was employed as a ballast van on engineers' trains; seldom used in normal service, it spent most of its time around Rolvenden yard. Note (left) the underframe of an R. Y. Pickering bogie carriage. *Author's collection*

Below:
Locomotive No 3 shunts brake van No 24 at Rolvenden *c*1937. This view features the van from the other (non-verandah) end and also shows to good effect the body details. *Author's collection*

Goods wagons and miscellaneous stock

Above:
Among a line of derelict carriages two cattle vans stand awaiting their final fate. The company purchased five cattle vans over the years — two Great Eastern, two North Eastern and one SECR. An ex-North Eastern and an ex-Great Eastern example are seen at Rolvenden on 26 March 1938. *R. F. Roberts*

Below:
A works photograph of Hurst Nelson four-plank open wagon No 1 *c*1899, showing the original Rother Valley lettering and livery. *Author's collection*

Above:
A family outing in a Fiat open tourer *c*1930. In the background are treasures of a different kind: behind the lady with the Scottie dog is Hurst Nelson four-plank open No 1, built in 1899 as one of 10 such wagons for the Rother Valley Railway, while behind the car is the underframe of a Pickering bogie carriage. *Lens of Sutton collection*

Below:
One of four ex-LBSCR five-plank open wagons purchased from the Southern Railway in 1940 to replace Hurst Nelson opens that had been condemned as life-expired. They were numbered 1-4. *R. S. Carpenter collection*

Above:
The R. Y. Pickering crane purchased in 1905.
It had a 5-ton lifting capacity and survived
until 1948 in use on engineering trains and
timber traffic at Frittenden Road. *Author's
collection*

Left:
The line's second crane was a substantial
six-wheel machine with a 10-ton lifting
capacity, purchased in 1919 from the
Midland Railway. This photograph, taken
*c*1929, shows it sandwiched between two
of the cattle vans in Rolvenden goods yard;
the building beyond the ex-North Eastern
cattle van (furthest from the camera) is the
printing hut. *R. F. Roberts*

Below:
Another view of the Midland six-wheel crane,
again at Rolvenden, this time in July 1938.
Author's collection

Above:
The Midland crane in store at Tenterden Town *c*1947. This photograph shows the crane, its runner, one of the ex-LBSC open wagons and two derelict runner wagons. Both cranes would be withdrawn for scrap by British Railways in 1948. *Lens of Sutton collection*

Below:
Gangers' pump trolley at Northiam on 8 April (Good Friday) 1955. These pump trolleys were in extensive use on the line throughout its existence. *R. F. Roberts*

The line after Nationalisation

Above:
Ex-LSWR '0395' 0-6-0 goods No 30576 prepares to leave Headcorn Junction with a solitary ex-LSWR bogie Corridor Brake Composite forming the service for Tenterden Town on 5 June 1948. The '0395s' were often used in the years 1945-8 as substitutes for 'O1s', this example being a frequent performer. *R. S. Carpenter collection*

Below:
Class 0395 0-6-0 No 30576 stands at Rolvenden on 5 June 1948 after working its part of the afternoon through train to Robertsbridge Junction. A Class A1X 'Terrier' 0-6-0T will replace it for the next leg of the journey along the Rother Valley. *R. S. Carpenter collection*

Above & below:
One of the problems associated with the line's operation: a Class A1X 'Terrier' and a long mixed train hold up traffic while a van on the train is unloaded of some crated goods at Rolvenden in the winter of 1952/3. Note the steel open wagon (second from left in the lower picture), which appears to be a rebuilt MoS SNCF-type four-wheel open, with end doors and flap-type side doors. *Photos from the Fifties*

Left:
A regular on the line in BR days, Class A1X 'Terrier' 0-6-0T No 32655 (now preserved on the Bluebell Railway in East Sussex) arrives at Rolvenden with a mixed train for Tenterden in December 1953. Note the ex-SECR 'Birdcage' brake carriage next to the locomotive. *Photos from the Fifties*

Below left:
Class O1 0-6-0 No 31064 heads a Rolvenden–Headcorn Junction mixed train between High Halden Road and Biddenden in the summer of 1953. *Author's collection*

Right:
Bathed in afternoon sunshine, No 31064 emerges from the darkness of St Michael's Tunnel with a Rolvenden–Headcorn Junction train consisting of a single ex-LSWR bogie brake in the summer of 1953. *Author's collection*

Below:
A general view of Rolvenden from a telegraph pole in the summer of 1953. Unusually it shows some activity at the shed, with No 31064 simmering in the platform while waiting to go on shed and 'Terrier' No 32655 blowing off on the shed road. The first 16-ton open mineral wagon is of interest by dint of its marked MoT reference to the Ministry of Transport. *Author's collection*

Last trip from Headcorn Junction

Taken on a dull Saturday in December 1953, the following pictures sum up the mood at the time of closure to passengers of the line

Above:
The changeover of the line's 'O1' class 0-6-0, which normally happened on a Saturday morning. No 31064 arrives for its duties on the line while No 31065 prepares to leave to return to Tonbridge shed for servicing after its stint on the KESR. *Photos from the Fifties*

Left:
The view east from the footbridge at Headcorn Junction station, with the London–Dover main line on the left and the Kent & East Sussex line, with its curved platform and series of loop sidings, on the right. *Photos from the Fifties*

Above right:
The yard at Headcorn Junction, viewed from the opposite direction. No 31064 simmers next to the signalbox, while at the platform is ex-LSWR Composite that will form the 10.55am to Tenterden Town. *Photos from the Fifties*

Right:
In the winter's gloom the 'O1' 0-6-0 and its single brake carriage hurry away from High Halden station and on towards St Michael's Halt and Tenterden Town. *Photos from the Fifties*

Above:
Having arrived at Tenterden Town No 31064 runs around its carriage using the loop. *Photos from the Fifties*

Left:
A photograph showing the two platforms at Tenterden Town station, with the 'O1' shunting in the coal yard in the distance. *Photos from the Fifties*

Below:
A photograph taken from the north end of the station in the direction of Robertsbridge, with the single carriage awaiting the return of the locomotive for the rest of its journey to Rolvenden. *Photos from the Fifties*

Above:
No 31064 arrives at Rolvenden from Tenterden Town with its train of one carriage at 12.15pm. This last part of the journey was not in the public timetable. *Photos from the Fifties*

Right:
The train at Rolvenden station after its protracted journey from Headcorn Junction. *Photos from the Fifties*

Below:
A general view of Rolvenden yard after No 31064 had shunted its carriage into the sidings and retired to the shed. *Photos from the Fifties*

Last day of passenger services

Above:
Headed by Class A1X 'Terrier' No 32655, the 9.38am from
Tenterden Town arrives at Robertsbridge on Saturday
2 January 1954, the last day of passenger services.
The train consists of an ex-SECR 'Birdcage' brake and an
ex-LSWR corridor Brake Composite. *Author's collection*

Above right:
No 32655 makes its way in spirited fashion across the Rother Levels
between Northiam and Wittersham Road with the 12.30pm from
Robertsbridge. Just visible in the background is the village of
Newenden. *Author's collection*

Right:
Class O1 0-6-0 No 31065 arrives at Rolvenden with a two-carriage
set of ex-LSWR bogie corridor brake vehicles forming the 8.50am
train from Headcorn. *Author's collection*

Above:
The final morning at Tenterden Town station. Taken in the direction of Headcorn Junction in cold winter sunshine, the photograph affords a fine view of the platforms and infrastructure. *S. Cartwright*

Below:
Biddenden station in the gloom of a winter's afternoon, as locals, including the village TA unit, turn out to say goodbye to their line.
S. Cartwright

Above:
In a rare double-heading of a single ex-LSWR corridor brake, 'O1' No 31064 and 'Terrier' No 32678 wait to depart Headcorn Junction for Tenterden Town and Rolvenden. Nos 32655 and 32678 would later work 'top and tail' on the last train from Tenterden Town to Robertsbridge Junction. *Author's collection*

Below:
In gathering twilight the very last train from Robertsbridge Junction, headed by No 32678 and banked by No 32655, enters Rolvenden on its final journey to Headcorn Junction; there 'O1' No 31064 will take over from the leading 'Terrier', No 32655 continuing to bank the six-carriage train to St Michael's Halt. *Author's collection*

Freight-only

Above left:
The last passenger train has long since departed from Tenterden Town as 'Terrier' No 32678 prepares to return to Robertsbridge Junction with the afternoon freight, consisting of an ex-LNER standard van and a Southern Maunsell brake van, in the summer of 1954. The boy on the platform looks rather forlorn, probably bemoaning the lack of interesting locomotives at his local station. *D. Lawrence*

Left:
No 32670, ex-Kent & East Sussex Railway No 3, steams through the remains of Rolvenden yard with a freight for Robertsbridge Junction in the summer of 1956, a year after the demolition of the station building and the locomotive shed. Built by the old company in 1946, the large water tower incorporates the underframe of steam rail car No 6 (built by Pickering in 1906), which spent most of its life rusting in the bushes at the back of Rolvenden yard. *N. Simmons*

Above:
Bodiam station in the mid-1950s, showing signs of neglect with its weed-grown platform and abandoned oil drums. The station still has its oil lamps and home starter signal now out of use. The signal would later be purchased by an enthusiast and is now preserved. *Hugh Davies*

Right:
Class A1X 'Terrier' No 32636 makes a spirited start from Tenterden Town with the return working of the Branch Line Society special from Robertsbridge to Tenterden Town on 12 April 1958. From 1954 until the final closure of the remaining Rother Valley section from Robertsbridge to Tenterden Town in June 1961 British Railways ran occasional special trains for hop-pickers on Sundays in the autumn (and for railway enthusiasts at other times); these would normally require a 'Terrier' at each end of the train. *N. Lera*

Dismantling of the Headcorn Extension

Above:
Class O1 0-6-0 No 31064, sporting an SPL19 headcode, simmers in the autumn sun as the demolition men from George Cohen & Co load another bogie bolster wagon of recovered track material at Biddenden. This station was used as a base to store material recovered from the line as it was lifted from north of Tenterden Town station to Biddenden. Dismantling of this section of line started in the summer of 1955 and was completed in December of that year. *Author's collection*

Left:
Later the same day No 31064 eases forward out of the abandoned goods yard with an empty bogie bolster wagon and runs towards the main line to Headcorn. The bolster wagon in the foreground is the next to be taken up to the junction with its load of bullhead rail, while the closed abandoned station in the background bathes in the afternoon sun. *Author's collection*

Below:
No 31064 stands in the platform at Biddenden with an ex-LMS 20-ton brake van and a train of bogie bolster wagons. The yard at Biddenden was used to sort materials for scrap or reuse. *Author's collection*

Top:
Bathed in summer evening sunshine in the late 1950s, the abandoned station at High Halden awaits passengers and trains that will never return. *D. Lawrence*

Above:
In the summer of 1962, seven years after the lifting of the Headcorn extension and eight years after the last passenger train, Biddenden station stands forlorn, weed-choked and trackless, left to slumber with only its ghosts and memories. *J. L. Smith*

Right:
As afternoon slowly makes way for evening, it is time for the 5.10pm to Headcorn Junction, which last ran 15 years ago. The end of the line at Tenterden Town in the summer of 1962. *J. L. Smith*

Last year of the Rother Valley Line

Left:
Tenterden Town looking towards Headcorn on 25 July 1960, just under a year before closure. The track is well kept and the station newly painted in this picture, which shows the MoS wartime Nissen huts on the far left. Note that the island platform is now gone. *David Knapman*

Below left:
A weed-strewn Northiam station in early June 1961, only weeks before final closure to all traffic. This was the view towards Robertsbridge. *David Knapman*

Above right:
A photograph of Northiam station from the rear, showing its newly painted exterior — which in BR days often seemed to presage closure! *David Knapman*

Right:
Shortly after the last photograph was taken Drewry 204hp 0-6-0 diesel shunter No D2276 arrived with the afternoon freight from Tenterden to Robertsbridge, here seen crossing the road. *David Knapman*

Below:
The guard of the short freight offered the photographer and a friend a ride to Robertsbridge, which was enthusiastically accepted. Here we see the goods yard at Northiam looking towards Tenterden. The goods yard is still full of coal wagons, despite imminent closure. *David Knapman*

Above:
A desolate but newly painted Bodiam station, photographed in the direction of Tenterden. Note that the oil drums are still on the platform. *David Knapman*

Left:
The view back from the brake van at a very derelict Junction Road Halt. *David Knapman*

Below:
Milepost 8, near Junction Road Halt, June 1961. *David Knapman*

Above:
No D2276 and its train rumble over the culvert bridge (of which there were many on the KESR) near Hudson's Mill, Robertsbridge, the guard having suggested to David and his friend that they leave the train here rather than continue into Robertsbridge station. Note the remains of the water tower and the wind pump. *David Knapman*

Below:
The Robertsbridge home signal is pulled off and the short freight heads off towards the junction, almost for the last time. *David Knapman*

Above:
The very last BR freight train over the Rother Valley line, hauled by a Drewry 0-6-0 diesel shunter, at Bodiam on the morning of 10 June 1961. This type had been used on the freight service from 1957, since when 'Terriers' had made only occasional forays up the line, when the diesels were being repaired at St Leonards depot. *N. Lera*

Left:
Closure notice at Robertsbridge station. *N. Lera*

Below:
The very last British Railways passenger train to work the line, on 11 June 1961, seen here at Rolvenden on its return working to Robertsbridge with 'Terrier' No 32670 at its head. This was, of course, entirely appropriate, as No 32670 was formerly Kent & East Sussex Railway No 3 *Bodiam* and was the only surviving locomotive from the old company. Note the Pullman car, third carriage from the locomotive; both this and a sister Restriction 0 Pullman have been purchased and preserved by the Kent & East Sussex Railway Preservation Society and are in use on 'wine and dine' trains. *N. Lera*